Thomas Dixon

Living problems in religion and social science

Thomas Dixon
Living problems in religion and social science
ISBN/EAN: 9783337718831
Printed in Europe, USA, Canada, Australia, Japan
Cover: Foto ©Lupo / pixelio.de

More available books at **www.hansebooks.com**

LIVING PROBLEMS

IN

RELIGION AND SOCIAL SCIENCE

BY

THOMAS DIXON, JR., M.A.,

PASTOR OF THE TWENTY-THIRD STREET BAPTIST CHURCH, NEW YORK CITY;
LATE OF THE DUDLEY STREET CHURCH, BOSTON.

NEW YORK
CHARLES T. DILLINGHAM
(SUCCESSOR TO LEE, SHEPARD & DILLINGHAM)
NOS. 718 AND 720 BROADWAY
1889

COPYRIGHT, 1889,
BY THOMAS DIXON, JR.

All Rights Reserved.

PRESS OF
THE PUBLISHERS' PRINTING COMPANY,
157-159 WILLIAM STREET,
NEW YORK.

Dedicated

TO MY WIFE,

IN WHOSE DEAR PERSON THE DAY-DREAMS AND IDEALS OF
MY BOYHOOD

LIVE AS THE SWEETEST REALITIES OF MANHOOD,

THE INSPIRATION OF WHOSE LOVE,

AS THE VOICE OF GOD,

CALLED ME

FROM THE VALLEY OF THE WORLD'S AMBITIONS

TO THE HEIGHTS OF NOBLER AIMS,

UNTO HER, WITH TENDEREST LOVE, THIS BOOK I BRING,

A SHEAF FROM THE FIRST FRUITS OF THAT
BETTER LIFE.

PREFATORY NOTE.

THESE condensed sermons and addresses are given to the public, with the hope and prayer that they may prove as helpful to a wide circle of readers as they seem to have been to those who first heard them delivered *extempore*. The treatment I have tried to make fresh and suggestive, rather than profound, or exhaustive. I owe much to the great thinkers of ancient and modern times; but what I have used from them, I trust has first passed through, and become a part of, my own heart and life. The addresses on current questions of Social Science were delivered before mass meetings in Boston and New York.

T. D., JR.

NEW YORK, Oct. 10, 1889.

CONTENTS.

		PAGE
1.	The Mission of the Church,	1
2.	The Minister's Sphere,	27
3.	Man vs. Fate,	50
4.	The Question of Hell,	71
5.	Miracles and Robert Elsmere; The Presumption Against a Miracle,	83
6.	Miracles and Robert Elsmere: The Question of Evidence,	97
7.	The Mystery of Pain,	110
8.	Progress,	129
9.	Playing the Fool: Or, the Problem of Folly,	144
10.	What is Love?	158
11.	The Temperance Problem,	167
12.	Jesuitism,	189
13.	The School War,	211
14.	The Southern Question,	244

LIVING PROBLEMS
In Religion and Social Science.

THE MISSION OF THE CHURCH.

As the Father hath sent me, even so send I you.—JOHN, xx. 21.

THE last act of our Master on earth was thus to lay the mantle of his mission on our shoulders. Sublime honor it is, and yet one freighted with sublimer responsibility.

Christ says to the Church: "You are the instruments of my will—the medium through which I shall operate on the world. My work is your work. What I came into the world to do I leave unto you to complete. My mission is your mission." To understand our own work, then, we turn, for a moment to the Master's life and learn the import of His mission. We will take these definitions from His own lips. I take several of the principal ones given in the record. In John, xii. 47: "I came not to judge the world, but to *save* the *world.*" In Luke, xix. 10: "The Son of Man *came to seek* and to save that which was lost." In Mark, ii. 17: "I *came not* to call the righteous, but the sinners." In Matthew, xx. 28: "The Son of Man came not to be ministered unto, but to minister."

You observe in these definitions certain negative facts. Let us first remove these negatives in order that we may give a clear conception of the positive elements of our mission. John and Mark say: "Came *not* to *judge* the world," "*not* to call the righteous." That is, Christ says: "My work is constructive rather than destructive. I am the way, the truth and the life, but I do not sit in harsh, censorious judgment on your acceptance or rejection of me. The Father is now judge. I am not come to judge, but to save." So he says to us: Judge not, but preach, proclaim, work, for the night is coming. As the Father was then the judge —not Christ—so Christ is now the judge, while we are to fill his former place. And if he did not come to call the righteous, it is impossible that his Church should be a ferryboat specially chartered to take a specified number of the fortunate elect from this world to the next. Nor is it a special car chartered for the special purpose of transporting the saints to heaven without contamination from the world. Yet, simple as is this lesson, it seems to be one of the hardest for our churches to learn. Yes, all of us, from the little mission church up to the great stone pile on the corner of the avenue, we are more or less impregnated with the idea that we are here to *get* rather than to *give*. That we are here to collect, to hoard up all the good we can out of the world, rather than to give out to struggling, dying sinners health and warmth and light and life and strength and love—that we may make the world brighter and gladder because we are here.

Again, says Matthew: "The Son of Man came not to be ministered unto, but to minister." And yet the majority of us think we are here to be ministered unto. Here is somebody who brings a letter to the church and joins, and in a month or two is ready to go elsewhere. What is the matter? "Well, I came to the church two months ago, and nobody has been to see us, no one has shown us any attention—any consideration at all!" So you want to go? Well, may joy go with you and peace reign behind you, for if you came into the church to receive attention, to be petted, to be ministered unto, the sooner you go the better for you and the better for the church of Christ. These are the sort of people who make up the *adherents* of a church. "How many adherents have you?" we sometimes hear asked. The Lord save the church from adherents! All that is necessary to sink a ship—any ship—the mightiest Cunarder that ploughs the waves—is to allow a sufficient number of adherents to become attached to her sides. Very little barnacles they may be, but enough of them will sink her as surely as if you had cut a hole in her bottom.

Then how many of our dear, good church members think that we are here to be fed simply.

Their religion consists in *being fed*. And they want it done just right, too. They want the napkin adjusted about their Sunday clothes, and then the milk administered with a spoon —condensed milk, too, all cream and fresh. They want it just so warm and no warmer— not hot; just so cool—not cold. But I imagine I hear some good old patriarch in Israel saying: "So, so, my young brother; but don't the Master say to you, 'Feed my sheep?'" Ah, yes, He does exactly! And how do you feed a sheep? When you feed a sheep do you back him up in a cushioned stall, carefully seat him, put a napkin about his neck, and feed him on milk with a spoon? I never saw it after that fashion. No. The shepherd took his flock out in the open fields, carpeted with rich grasses; on the hillsides and mountain tops, where they browsed on the budding shrubbery, so that sufficient exercise is taken to properly digest and assimilate what is eaten. So should the pastor lead his flock to this great Book. Here are broad, rich fields and smiling meadows, through which runs the laughing brook; yonder lies the long range of hills, and yonder lies the mountain crag, whose summits the eye of man cannot measure, for they are lost amid the azure blue of heaven, while below lie green pastures beside still and beautiful waters. Here is food in abundance; take and eat.

Having thus set aside these negative elements, we come to the positive ones in the Master's and our own mission. The remaining elements in these definitions can all be condensed into a single positive proposition, to which let us address ourselves. What, then, is the positive mission of the Master, and, therefore, our mission? *"The Son of Man came to seek and to save that which is lost—to save the world."*

I. The first element—*The Son of Man came to seek.* Alas, how often we forget this. Most of us seem to think our active duty is done when we have built a church, paid for it, opened its doors and invited the lost to come by writing a sign over the door and an advertisement in the paper.

Let us see what the Master says: A certain man made a great feast and issued the proclamation, Come, for all things are now ready. But they began to make excuses. One had bought a field, the other a yoke of oxen, and another had married; and there were empty seats at the supper. Then, said the Master to the servants, "Go out quickly into the streets and lanes of the city and bring in hither the poor, and maimed and blind." And they said, "It is done, Lord, and yet there is room." Then go out into the highways and hedges and constrain them to come in that my house may be filled.

Are there ever vacant seats in this church on the Lord's Day? Then it is your fault. Hear the voice of Jesus crying, Go out into the highways and hedges and constrain them to come in! I care not how beautiful the house, how soft the cushions in the pews, it is not pleasing unto God unless those seats are filled with throbbing human hearts. And you, the rank and file of the church, are responsible if it is so, for this commission was given to the rank and file, the common priesthood of believers.

Constructed on some modern ideas of church work how would the parable of the lost sheep read? Somewhat thus: And a certain man, when he found that some of his sheep were lost, went out near the wilderness and built a handsome sheep shelter, and on the door wrote the sign, "Any lost sheep straying near this wilderness hard by, if he will present his credentials, and give good references to the committee in charge, will be admitted to shelter after due deliberation and examination and consultations." Did the Master say this? No! But the shepherd went out on the mountains wild and bare,

"And although the road was rough and steep,
 He goes to the desert to find the sheep,
 But none of the ransomed ever knew
 How dark was the night that the Lord passed through
 Ere He found His sheep that was lost.
 Out in the desert He heard its cry,
 Sick and helpless and ready to die.
'Lord, whence are those blood drops all the way,
 That mark out the mountain's track?'
 They were shed for one who had gone astray
 Ere the Shepherd could bring him back.

> But all through the mountains thunder-riven,
> And up from the rocky steep,
> There arose a cry to the gates of Heaven,
> 'Rejoice! for I have found my sheep!'
> And the angels echo round the throne,
> 'Rejoice, for the Lord brings back His own!'"

Such was his divine mission—such is yours. The Son of Man came to *seek* that which was lost! "As the Father hath sent me even so send I you." Remember that Christ spoke that sentence not to the twelve apostles simply, but to all the disciples assembled—to the whole church, to *you*. Do not think that you can do this work by proxy. Some people think that they hire a minister to do their duties to God. It cannot be done, my friend. You cannot delegate your own personal duties to some one else. I cannot perform the duties of the least child in my church. Each one must give an account of himself unto God. I have my work, and you have yours.

II. The second element—"*And to save that which is lost.*" Yes, it would be a pity to bring them in from the highways and hedges and from the mountains, and then let them perish, let them starve. So this church of Christ is to be a *saving* church. And to have this saving quality it must be *a praying church*, whose members know how to bring their burdens, their joys, their sorrows to the Lord, and tell all life's stories to Him; in whose hearts and lives the Holy Spirit dwells because they are ready to receive the Spirit; a church that answers its own prayers as far as human power can go, and then asks God in faith to do the rest, and He does. He never does anything we can do ourselves.

When Christ stood before the grave of Lazarus he commanded those men to roll the stone away! Why did he not roll it himself by supernatural power? Because it could be done by natural power. Then he called forth the dead and said, "Loose the grave clothes;" again commanding that man do that which need not call forth supernatural effort. So the Lord never answered the prayer of the old sinner who prayed that He would feed the poor, when his own corn crib was bursting with grain and he would not give a nubbin.

The saving church is always the sacrificing church—ready to sacrifice *money* and *manhood*. Money! God is not poor. The wealth of the universe is His. Not because of His poverty or weakness does He command us to give, but for our own benefit, because it is a sweet privilege.

A poor widow lay dying the other day in one of the back streets of one of our great cities. The only soul near was her little ragged boy, and as he gazed into the dying face, she said, "Do not be afraid, my boy, God will take care of you!" Two days later that boy, who had not tasted food in all that time, stood shivering and gazing appealingly into the faces of the throng that hurried by. He asked a gentleman for a penny, told him his sad story, took him by the hand and led him down into the squalid home where the dead body lay on a pile of rags. The gentleman took the boy home, adopted him and cared for him as his own. God had cared for him, but He had honored that man by making him a co-worker in a divine mission. So does He honor us with the privilege of giving.

The man who refuses to give to the cause of Christ is not a Christian. He need not tell me about his religion—he has none. A man who has faith in God will invest in God. A man who is converted is ready to help on the work. What would you think if a man were drowning out in the river, and you should set out in your boat to rescue him, and, pulling with might and main, reach him in time to lift him in the boat and save him. Then suppose you say to him, "I am tired and weak from the heavy struggle. Will you please take an oar and help as we pull for the shore?" And the man says, "Excuse me. I thought this was a free salvation. You put me in this boat, now I'll let you row me ashore!" What ought you to do with such a man? What could you do except seize him by the nape of the neck and the heels and plunge him as near the bottom as you could? *Save* such a man? How could you? Nothing there to save!

But money is not the only thing or the most important thing we are called on to give. Money, after all, is easy to get, but the thing that counts and that God demands above all things else is your manhood and womanhood, your individuality, yourself, your living, throbbing personality. I know a man worth a million who at the beginning of the year draws his check for a thousand dollars, hands it to his church treasurer and says: "Take this, do what you please with it—but don't trouble me any more this year about anything!" I tell you, my friend, God does not want your money in that way. He wants *you!* Your time, your care, your personality.

And then the saving church is one that knows how to use the Word. This Word is the great weapon given you by which the world is to be conquered. If you do not know how to wield it how can you dare enter? Two fools met near Paris recently and fought a duel. Suppose one of them had known nothing of the use of the sword, you would have pronounced him mad! Do you know how to use the sword? Do you know how to parry a blow with it? Do you know its temper, its capacity? Do you know how to strike? How to defend yourself, and how to thrust its glittering blade into the marrow of the foe? To be a saving church we must know something of this.

III. The third element—what is to be saved—*That which is lost.* "The Son of Man came to seek and to save that which is lost." What is lost? What an atmosphere of horror clings to that word "lost," to its accent, intonation, every letter! The human heart leaps in pity and terror at the sound. *Lost!*

A few years ago the news was flashed over the wires to the uttermost limits of the earth that a little, curly-haired boy named Charlie Ross was *lost!* And a world was thrilled with horror at the thought! Oh, how many loving mothers woke in the morning, looked into the faces of their own dear little ones, while a tear filled the eye as they thought of that desolate home! How eagerly we read the papers, watching and waiting for some news from the lost one. *Lost!* Each letter drips with condensed horror! What is lost? Lost—a world! Swinging somewhere in space between the planets Venus and Mars—lost a world! Not simply one boy or girl, but millions of bright-eyed boys and girls, noble boys and girls, noble men and women, *lost*, wandering in the wilderness of sin, exposed to a thousand dangers of body and soul; out in the deserts, bleak and bare; on mountain crags, wild and trackless; sick and helpless and ready to die! O God, can Thy children be indifferent to such a mission! How the thought should thrill the soul with divine heroism! Can any man slumber with such a work upon him? But how are we to save the world?

If it is to be done the slumbering power of our churches must be developed. The whole church must be up and doing—not simply the little church within the church. There is always an old guard in every church, on which the pastor can always depend, and they generally do nearly everything, but if this mighty work is to be accomplished it is to be done by the rank and file all bearing their part in the conflict. How long would it take the Baptist churches alone to take the world for Christ if each one of us who profess His name should bring one new soul into the kingdom each year—a little thing to do—just bring one soul to Christ in a whole year. And yet, if we could only do that, the Baptist churches alone could take this world for Christ in less than nine years—yes, every continent of earth, every island of the seas, every nation, every tongue, every tribe that inhabits the globe! Yet, how few of us do this? Oh, how many church members we have who are buried beneath cushioned pews and gilded walls; buried beneath stone and cement and glittering spires; buried! and buried alive! Oh, the crime of it!

If this work is to be done we must realize, too, that Christianity is revolutionary and means war, and work. You have entered upon a tremendous conflict! The very mission of your belief is as terrible as an army with banners. You should go forth to this battle armed and all in trim, with head erect and eye fixed upon the foe. Go with the conscious tread of a conscious conqueror knowing that the Lord of heaven and earth is at your right hand.

This Christian warfare can never be waged successfully on the hospital idea. What army ever achieved victory that made its hospital the foremost portion of its work. Suppose Gen. Grant, during those last days of terrific carnage, had said to his army of 200,000 men, "I detail the flower of this army to hospital service. We have 10,000 men who have the measles and the mumps, and several thousand wounded. We will now nurse them before any more fighting is done. I will spend my time tying up stubbed toes and picking splinters out of men's fingers! Charge on the hospitals!" Had you run the Northern army on that principle it would have taken Lee just about ten days to have dictated terms of peace from the White House steps.

Some of us think that the church is built for purposes of defence simply. The church is no fort behind which shivering cowards are to crouch. It is not built for defensive but aggressive warfare.

During the battle of Manassas, it is said that an officer passing over the field found a subordinate crouching behind a haystack trembling from head to foot. Coming up to the spot, he asked: "What sort of a place is that for you, sir?" When he was greeted with the eager reply, "Do—why, do you really think the bullets can come through?" In the thought of personal safety the poor coward had lost the conception of the very object of his commission. Sometimes weak-kneed Christians come to me with the question, "Do you think I am safe? Do you think the bullets can come through?" What? come through the church wall? No, I do not *think* anything about it. I *know* it! The devil can get you off this front seat just as easily as from the back one —can take you out of the pulpit just as easily as off the door steps.

To accomplish such a mission means work as well as war—hard work, some of it dirty work. I know some Christians, though, who are the nicest sort of people, but they do not want to soil their hands with the rough work. Oh, those dainty hands! Lord help us. Crows, here we live spending our time smoothing our dark feathers. Crows, we know we are, and yet expect to some day suddenly blossom out in heaven in the shape of nightingales and astonish the celestial hosts with our wonderful voices. The choir will cease its divine melody, while one angel looks at the other and exclaims, "What is that?" I am afraid Christians are not translated into heaven by that process.

I am afraid something is the matter if we are too nice to do the Lord's work! For there was a day when Christ, the King of kings, and Lord of lords, descended from the royal throne of the Heavens, laid aside His diadem that outshone the sun, laid aside the jeweled sceptre of the universe, and came down to this wicked old world,—down through all grades of society He came, from the highest to the lowliest, shedding joy and light and life as He came. He stooped to save even the lowest wretch—yes down in the lowest depths of life's darkest and meanest prison cell He came, and then reached out His hand to the guilty, tattered wretch who lay there and said: "My Brother, I have come all the way from heaven to earth to save you!"

What sort of church would we have if these principles were carried out?

1. Such a church would be liberal. A mean, stingy man couldn't stay in it. There would be much bustle and stir, energy and power—in short, too much life. It would shatter his nerves. He never could stand it. He would have nervous prostration. He would leave so easily you wouldn't know he had gone. He would fold his tent like an Arab and silently steal away!

2. Such a church would be united always, standing shoulder to shoulder with a single grand thought ever before them, and moving toward that end in a solid phalanx. Such unity, too, would be genuine. Not such a unity as an old deacon once affirmed of his church. They had been distracted by terrible factions and divisions. His friend asked him one day: "Well, deacon, how are you getting on, now?" "Well, we are united at last." "Is it possible. How did it come about?"

"Frozen! frozen through from top to bottom, solid as a rock." No, not such a unity as that, but a union such as is made by laying one piece of red-hot iron on another, and striking across the anvil until welded as one piece that will stand the suns of summer, the winds and snows of a thousand winters

3. Such a church, too, would be a joyous one. It would not be filled with moping, shivering, doubting Christians. Have you a joyous religion, my friend? If not, go bring some lost sinner into the fold and taste and see that the Lord is good. I have not been in the service long, but nothing can rob me of the joy of some of its hours. I remember one night, when I first entered the work, and was preaching in Raleigh, there came into the inquiry room after the sermon an old man of about sixty. He was a stranger to me, and apparently to everybody else but an elderly gentleman who accompanied him. He seemed in the greatest distress imaginable. I began to talk with him and try to show him the way of life. He groaned and turned from side to side as though

he were choking or smothering. At last he exclaimed, "O my young friend, I've been working on this problem forty years and I can't see it!" "Well," I said, "you have been working on it forty years, and it's too hard a problem—you can't work it out. Suppose, now, you give it all to Christ, and let Him work it out for you." I turned and left him and had not walked five steps before he leaped up with a shout that made the very building ring as he fell on the neck of his old friend and cried like a child for very joy. I can see him yet, with the great tears rolling down his furrowed cheeks, his gray locks streaming back from his upturned face, that seemed lit by the light of heaven. He went out from that room into the darkness of the night, and I never saw him again; but no power on earth can rob me of the joy of that hour or its memory, for I expect to meet him some day within the golden gates.

Christian friends, will you not consecrate yourselves to this glorious work? There is a work for you. Be up and doing. Ah, you say you are weak and timid and unfit for the Master's service. Not so! Your very weakness and helplessness God makes the instrument through which He will display His power and majesty. Besides you are not too weak—the smallest child, the feeblest old woman has her work.

An old negro washerwoman was walking along the railroad track near Louisville, Ky., one morning just after daybreak going to her day's work, when just in front of her, she observed the bridge that spanned a deep ravine had burned away in the night. The rails only remained stretching treacherously across the gulf. She remembered that the early express was about due, and with all haste started back to the little station a mile away to give the alarm. She had not gone more than a few hundred yards before she heard the roar of the coming train, and in a moment more the great engine swept round the curve just in front of her. She tried to tear her apron from her waist for a signal—the string seemed never so strong and stubborn as then, but at last she tore it loose and waved it frantically, determined to stand on that track and die or stop the train. At last she was seen, the engine reversed and brought to a stand only a few feet from her. The engineer thrust his head out the cab, and cried, "Well, old woman, are you crazy—what's the matter?" "Oh, sah, de bridge is all burned down, 'deed it is, sah,—you'll be lost if you go on!" The engineer leaped from his cab, and the passengers from the cars, and there before them saw the awful death they had barely escaped. Friend embraced friend, and mothers fell upon the necks of children as they realized their great deliverance. The old woman, as she saw their tears and joy, began to dance and shout for joy herself. They drew near her and offered her their money and jewelry, but she refused to touch a thing, saying she was afraid it would take her joy away for what she had been able to do, and went her way, with a light heart, to her day's work. You can do at least as much as that old woman. Down the track of life there comes thundering toward you some reckless man or woman.

You see the bridge is down, and the gulf yawns before them. They do not see it perhaps—at least you can stand on that track and with the blood-stained banner of Christ flag the coming train!

You may be weak and timid, but remember that success does not depend on your weakness or strength, but on God! A little child by touching a screw can in an instant flood a great building with the glare of an electric blaze. But what makes the light? The child? No. But there is at the central station a great dynamo, perhaps of 500 horse power, that sends from its throbbing heart the pulsing fire throughout the length and breadth of the city.

When the excavations at Hell Gate were completed after years of work, and the dynamite all in place and everything in readiness, it is said the engineer in charge called his little bright-eyed daughter to the table in his office and told her to explode the great mine. The tiny finger sought the black button, a gentle pressure and Manhattan Island trembled at the terrific shock, as the great boulders rose and lifted heavenward a mountain of foam-capped water.

So the tiny hand of a child, though weak and feeble, uplifted to God in prayer, touches the dynamo of the universe and may bring an answer that shakes the earth. God help us to remember Thy power and our duty!

THE MINISTER'S SPHERE.

"Whom we proclaim, admonishing and teaching every man in all wisdom."—COL. I. 28.

THE so-called "sacredness" of the office has never and never will oppress me. I am worth just as much as a minister as I am as a man, and no more. I weigh just as much as my heart and brain and personality weigh when put into the scales and weighed—not an ounce more, not an ounce less. The letters R E V that men put before my name add nothing to its weight. They mean nothing; they are nothing. If it were possible to put that title into a concrete particle and place it under a microscope that magnified a million diameters, the eye of man could never find it, if given eternity in which to look for it. It seems to me that Beecher is surely right when he maintains that here manhood only counts. My office is sacred, but sacred because my manhood is sacred. If I am mean and small and stingy and vicious, the sacredness of the office I hold in no wise furnishes a refuge for my weaknesses. If there is a deacon or a humble member of this church who has a bigger heart, a bigger brain and a greater personality than the pastor, then he is a more sacred man than I am, and is entitled by the divine right of that manhood to wield a greater influence than I can wield.

But let us go simply to the text for the true definition of the scope and function of the Christian minister.

WHOM.—We have in this first word, "whom," outlined the scope of the office. We see at once from the personal pronoun the very obvious fact that the substance of the message to be delivered through the minister is not a creed or fine-spun philosophy, but a person—the personality of Christ the Son of God, the Saviour of mankind. A life, then, we have, embodying the divine revelation; and we do not search for it in any mysterious system of metaphysics, but in the depths of the life thus revealed.

We are to preach, then, the personality of Jesus Christ—His life, His death, His resurrection, and all that clusters around Him. Now, it is precisely the purpose of the whole epistle to the Colossians to set forth this marvellous personality in its completeness, its fulness, its all-sufficient power. The church at Colossæ had become befogged in the fine-spun theories of would-be philosophers in their attempts to bridge the chasm between the material and the spiritual. They had peopled earth and heaven with their mysterious beings, semi-angelic, half spirit, half matter. Paul now comes and with the hand of a master brushes these useless creatures aside, and boldly sets forth Christ as the connecting link between matter and spirit, earth and heaven; Christ the way from earth to heaven; Christ in the light of his divine-human personality, filling the universe, material and immaterial; Christ, all and in all, whether of things on the earth, above the earth, or beneath it. Such is Paul's conception. He sees this wonderful personality encircling the world, touching the personality of man at every possible point of contact, and reaching up until He fills all heaven and touches the personality of God at every possible point of contact. To preach Christ, therefore, is to preach that which concerns all things, human and divine.

WE.—Whom does Paul include in this plural pronoun? Evidently those humble Christians, whoever they were, who had carried the Gospel to Colossæ. He does not arrogate to himself any special prerogatives or privileges because of his office, but simply places himself on the same level with those less distinguished followers of the Master who had first carried the glad tidings to the Colossians. Unquestionably, Paul seems here to have had a clear conception of the common priesthood of believers, and does not make any pretensions to the office of a papal legate, cardinal, or bishop. He speaks with authority—the authority of one who knows the mysteries of the glories of supreme truth; but does not claim to have any special patent on that truth. If, when men say the ministry should not interfere in public affairs, they mean a class clergy, an aristocracy, an ecclesiastical hierarchy, bound by common oaths for the advancement of their own ends, I, of course, agree at once; but not upon the ground of the sacredness of their office, but on the ground that they are a dangerous nuisance to the common weal of a nation of free men.

PROCLAIM.—This word *proclaim* introduces us to the first division of the definition of the function of the minister. He is to proclaim, to utter, to tell out a message. Not mumble mysterious ceremonies, go through idiotic services in an unknown tongue; not to offer sacrifices, masses, mummeries, or give utterance to vague whisperings in dark corners; but to openly proclaim a great message, before all men and under all circumstances. My heart has always said amen to Prof. Phelps's hearty exhortation to his students, when he says: "Preach; let other men govern. Preach; let other men organize. Preach; let other men raise funds and look after denominational affairs. Preach; let other men hunt up heresies and do the theological quibbling. Preach; let other men ferret out scandals and try clerical delinquents. Preach; let other men solve the problems of perpetual motion, of which church history is full. Then, make a straight path between your study and your pulpit, on which the grass shall never grow." To proclaim, then, with tongue and life this message, is the first function of the true minister of Christ. This is the work of the messenger. The boy who brings me the telegram has no right to alter, add to, or subtract from it. So with him who utters the fundamental truths of this message. These truths are simple, plain and yet ample for all needs. But is the minister simply a telegraph boy, and does his duty cease with the delivery of this simple message? If so, Paul should have closed his sentence with this word "proclaim." This he does not do, and we take it that in what follows he will further qualify and define the duties of the office, as we find he does.

The next words, "ADMONISHING and TEACHING," open a new field of action. This work of admonition and teaching is one of transcendent importance and is a vast expansion of the work of proclamation.

In the first place, a man who faithfully admonishes must be a man utterly fearless of mortal or devil; one was does not hesitate to tell those about him whether they are right or wrong, and that too in monosyllabic English, and without any attempt primarily to please the subject warned. Says Paul: "Am I still pleasing men? If I were still pleasing men, I would not be the servant of Christ?" If there is a man, woman or child in this church whom I am trying personally in my ministry to please, I don't know who it is. No minister of Christ has a right to attempt to please any man or set of men. The preacher who should attempt this would be a fool on general principles, for the simple reason that it is impossible to please man.

And then the word admonish blends the Old Testament conception of the watchman: "I have set watchmen on thy walls, O Jerusalem, and they shall never hold their peace, day or night!" The watchman is one who admonishes. He is watching, warning, and giving the proper signals to those over whom he is set as guardian; he should be sleepless, vigilant, with an ear attuned to every sound, and an eye whose keen vision sweeps the whole horizon from hour to hour. I know a good woman who recently said: "I had rather a child of mine would be a hod-carrier than a clergyman!" The statement struck me as an interesting one. I was curious to know what her conception of a clergyman was. And in a subsequent conversation with her, I think I caught her conception of an ideal minister. She was describing one whom she had once known and very much admired. The closing characterization of her sacred hero was that "he was such a *good* man!" And she tenderly and reverently accented the word good with lengthened sweetness long drawn out. That was her notion of an ideal minister. I felt like asking her in haste, "Has he made his will? He will die soon—he cannot be long for this world!" Alas, he had been dead some time.

When a minister has reached the period that such an expression accurately describes his life and work, it is time for him to go—he is too good to live here in this rickety old world of sin and devilment. For a goody-good preacher I have always entertained only pity and contempt. What a sublime calling, indeed, to go up and down in this world, patting everybody on the back with—"It's all right, everything's all right, everybody's all right, you're all right—the devil's all right!" Yes. I think I had rather my boy would go back to the old farm in North Carolina and grub stumps, maul rails, hoe corn, and plough a mule as did his father once, than be such a man —he would be doing more for his country, his God and the human race.

Paul was not a goody-good preacher. He generally raised a row in the towns he entered. They beat, they put him in prison. The enraged citizens seized him by the throat, dragged and pounded him up before the magistrates with the accusing exclamation: "These men who have turned the world upside down have come hither also!" and they demanded their immediate expulsion. They desired to kick him because he had turned things upside down. If he had been a *"good"* man only, they would have had no objection to him, simply because be would have amounted to nothing. Nor was Christ, though He was the impersonation of love, in any sense of the word a goody-good preacher. He came not to bring peace but a sword; but, the blade He wielded was the surgeon's knife, not the cimetar of the Saracen. When He stood before the scribes and Pharisees, He did not give them honeyed words. They were made very clearly to understand that they were hypocrites and scoundrels. He did not once mince matters with them. Hear Him: "Woe unto you, scribes and Pharisees, hypocrites! for ye are like unto whited sepulchres, which outwardy appear beautiful, but inwardly are foul of dead men's bones, and of all uncleanness." Christ never hesitated to faithfully admonish, when admonition was necessary. He did not tell them certainly that they were all right, everything and everybody all right.

There are many people in this world who object to this last phase of the preacher's work.

Here is a man who objects to being taught, because, as he says, he is an expert in his own business; and, therefore, knows more about it than any impertinent parson in the country. "What do you know about my business?" he indignantly asks. "Have I not spent a lifetime in it? How dare you interfere with your impudent criticism?" So says the skipper to Paul when reminded of the fact that he ought not to have loosed from Crete. I imagine I can hear that captain say: "What do you know about navigation, you miserable land lubber?" Now, the words Paul uttered were in nowise impertinent. He did not say: "You have no sense in the management of this boat! That sail is not set right!" He merely said: "You ought not to have started on this journey at such a time." He did not sit in judgment upon the technique of navigation, but simply gave an opinion of its relation to the world without—a matter of which he may have been a better judge than the captain, as subsequent events showed in fact that he was, for the result was they were wrecked and he had to take charge of the whole thing.

Here is a young Napoleon on the stock exchange, starting on the road that leads to Sing Sing. I warn him that he is gambling. Hear his indignant reply: "Gambling, indeed! What do you know about stocks and bonds? What do you know about this great business in which I am engaged? What do you know, you sacred fool, about commerce or the mechanism of exchange?" I reply, not much, perhaps. I don't need to know much about the mechanism of exchange in order to know the difference between an honest man and a thief or a gambler! To judge the technique of your trade, I have neither time nor inclination, but I do have the right, and I take the time, to judge of the relation of your business to the world of morals, and here I do claim to be even a better judge than you, for I at least am disinterested. Men complain sometimes that the preacher is too personal. That is just what I am here for. I am nothing, if not personal.

I always try to level the old musket so as to hit something. I never shoot blank cartridges, and if I do not hit somebody every fire, it is not because I do not try. Why should I stand up here and shoot at nothing from Sunday to Sunday? No! I propose to shoot at you in every relation of life, and you need not try to dodge amid the technicalities of your trades and shake at me your yard sticks, your hammers, or bank books. J. H. Mills, while editor of the *Biblical Recorder* in Raleigh, gave in his paper a severe criticism of an amateur musical performance, which so enraged the director of that eventful night's work that he retorted to the criticism in a heated public card, and wound up his tirade with the taunt, "It was better than you could have done!" To which the unruffled editor replied: "Granted. Your remark is true, but irrelevant. Any hen in this country can lay an egg. I cannot perform that feat; but I fearlessly maintain that I am still a better judge of eggs than every hen in North Carolina." The answer was complete.

I do not know the process of preparing beef steak, but I do know a good piece of steak when I see it and taste it. I do not understand the process of making flour, but I do know good bread when I see it. I do not understand the process of cooking, but I know a good dinner when I get to it. And I do not hesitate to inform my cook if it is not right. I do not know all the mysteries of banking and currency, but I do know the difference between honesty and dishonesty. Christ had never read Adam Smith, or Ricardo, or J. S. Mill, or even Aristotle and Plato. He did not know necessarily about the mechanism of exchange, but he did know enough to overturn the tables of the money changers in the temple and drive them from its sacred precincts.

Here is a politician, well fed, large in circumference, red nose, and luminous eyes, and loud breath. He has credentials of scores of delegates to a convention in his unhallowed pocket and obtained them by fraud. He manipulates things to suit himself, panders in his platform utterances to the lowest and vilest element of our life, and coolly demands that I vote for his man and his principles, and threatens to forever cast out of the synagogue all heretics who refuse to obey his supreme will. I say to him, you are a villain, sir! He replies with lofty scorn for my inexperience and ignorance. "What do you know about politics? What do you know about caucuses and conventions? What do you know about the machinery by which this great government is run?" Well, I don't know a great deal about caucuses, primaries, conventions and legislative bodies, but I do know a thief and a cut-throat when I see him. And I have the right to stand before him and his misdeeds.

Then there is a large class who delight to hear abstract truth uttered, but who shy at a personal application; and one of their pet cant phrases is "I want to hear the GOSPEL." That is, they want to hear a theoretical Christianity preached, and make the application to some other fellow at their leisure. They swallow as a sweet beverage the abstract, but fight like a child over medicine at the concrete. They shut their teeth and refuse to take it, and the first opportunity shout, "I want you to preach Christ!" They want the fundamentals proclaimed, but not applied. They will weep with you while you tell them of the one little ewe lamb, but when you say, "David, thou art the man!" they are sad. They wrap the drapery of a freezing dignity about them and retire, and send you word indirectly through a friend that they want to hear the "Gospel preached."

It has been well said that the gospel is the multiplication table of the science of religion. Here is our professor in mathematics. The class reaches this table. The professor says: "Well, gentlemen, we have reached the multiplication table this morning—it is a marvellous table, it is the key to the whole kingdom of mathematics. It never changes—it is always true. It is the same yesterday, to-day and forever. Each given proposition is the impersonation of an eternal truth. So marvellously true is this table that I have decided that we will repeat it forever. We will not try to go beyond this—we will simply repeat it forever." Of course that professor would lose his position, and so do a good many preachers, for about the same reason, I fear. As we press the multiplication table into the realm of algebra, geometry, trigonometry, calculus, and applied mathematics, so is the gospel of Christ to be pressed into every phase of human life, and its eternal standards of truth and right applied to all developments of human thought and conduct. I know an old deacon of a Baptist church who seriously objects to applied mathematics in the pulpit. He is worth about $30,000, and gives fifty cents a year to his church, and loans his pastor money at eight per cent interest. If his pastor preaches a sermon on giving, it lands the old man in the middle of a spell of sickness. He can squeeze a dollar so tight till it feels like a dime. He never tires hearing you tell how ten times ten make a hundred—that is glorious, sweet to him. But when you say ten dimes make a dollar, and a dollar is your share of the burden, my brother, you hurt his feelings. His countenance falls ten degrees below zero, and the sorrow of his countenance makes you wish you had not said anything. He is hurt. He turns in his mind to the choir and asks them to please sing, and there is just one song to which his wounded spirit turns, and that is, "I'm glad salvation's free!" He wants the whole chorus to come in on that word free. He wants to hear the bass, tenor, soprano, and alto just there, together with all the wind and stringed instruments. Just there he wants the cymbals, drum, and bass viols to come in, and the trombone man to let out his horn full length!

I know another member of the church, who is always sighing and crying for the "pure gospel." He drinks. He keeps a demijohn at home under the bed all the time, and takes it when he feels like it. Let his pastor preach on temperance, and you will hear from him! You will hear his voice crying in the land for the "pure gospel." That is, he wants to sit up in the amen corner, fold his arms and watch his pastor make the fur fly; but he does not want to furnish any of the fur. He wants to see it fly off common sinners, while his own grows long and silken and fine as he feeds on the "pure gospel."

I, of course, agree that the gospel is the thing to preach, but we are to remember that this gospel encircles the material universe, touching man at every possible point of contact, and fills all heaven with its glories. As a minister of this glorious gospel of Jesus Christ, it is my right and duty to take my surveyor's compass and chain out into the fields of the world's activities, survey by the unerring magnet the pathway man marks out for himself, and tell him whether it is straight or crooked, whether it is narrow and mean, or whether it is broad and generous. It is my work to drop the plumb line of God's truth down over the foundations of your character, and by my applied sacred mathematics to tell you whether it is square or crooked. By far the most important function of my work is this application of fundamental gospel truth to your every-day life and character. I have no right to preach anything with which the gospel is not concerned. In what is the gospel concerned? Anything and everything that is either right or wrong. Then, is there a single thought or deed possible to man with which this gospel has nothing to do? I have yet to hear of the principle, deed, or thought to which this gospel cannot apply. Surely, then, we are not to be goody-goodies. What is Paul's form of congratulation as he closes his life work? Does he say: "Thank God, I have never made an enemy; I have always been modest and gentle and kept within my sphere?" No! But hear the language of the veteran soldier: "I have fought a good fight!" So is it my duty to fight a good fight, and not to sugar-coat the world, the flesh, and the devil!

Such a work, therefore, as is here outlined is also necessarily preventive in its character, for the watchman who warns is one who gives the danger signal at its first approach. I bought a copy of an evening paper the other day, as I returned home, and the first thing upon which my eye fell was a dispatch from Providence saying that a drunken brute had gone home and demanded of his wife two dollars of her hard earnings, that he might return to the grog-shop and complete his drunk. This she refused, and thereupon, with the ferocity of a beast, he fell upon her and beat her to death; and, as she lay dying, she turned to her child and said: "My boy, run for Father Finnigan, quick!" Father Finnigan hastened to come; but she died before he reached the house, to go through his ceremonies over her dead body. Now, there are those who think that Father Finnigan's duty began and ended with his ceremonies over that body, but, as for me, I demand a religion that begins its work before the autopsy, or not at all. If I cannot come into the house before the undertaker, then I will not come at all; I will quit the business.

I look around me and see the devil mount the driver's box of our national life. I see him draw the reins over the arched necks of the political steeds harnessed to the national chariot. Each horse acknowledges the grip of the master. He lifts high those reins and brings down his lash on the bare backs of his high-tempered brutes. Forward they dash, obedient to his command. Madly onward they plunge, as the lash descends again and again. On, on they leap over throngs of helpless men, women and children. Their bodies are ground beneath the wheels and iron hoofs. Hear their sighs, groans, and shrieks as their blood in dark pools stains the pavements! Dismayed at the horrible sight, I cry aloud: "My God, cannot something be done?" About that time, I hear the squeaking voice of some little preacher as he hastens to say: "No, you can't do anything! Nothing can be done! You must stand out of the way, or you will get run over yourself. Besides, man, it would be out of place for you to attempt to do anything. You are specially set apart! Think of that! Just think of the cut of your coat! Think of the style of your collar!" In reply, I feel like crying: "Silence! You keep me from my thoughts. If that is all you have to say, let Nature's stillness be the only requiem of the dead that lie around us. I never wear a collar that chokes me. When my collar gets so high and stiff as to form an impassable barrier between me and the cause of humanity and God, then I will cut my collar down; and if it can't be cut down, I must take it off—I will not wear a collar—I will go out of the business."

A hard work it is often to wound that you may heal, to slay that life may be given; but it is the crowning glory of a life to be called of God to such a work.

MAN vs. FATE.

So then each one of us shall give an account of himself unto God.—ROM. xiv. 12.

CHRISTIANITY is yet burdened with the legacy of pagan theology. The astrology of the Chaldeans is still a potent force in too many lives. The Greek and Roman Fates wove their accursed threads not only into the web of ancient life, but through literature, philosophy, and religion, those three old hags are still spinning, weaving, and cutting the tangled threads of human destiny. Christ came and found the world trembling lest they frown. We are not yet freed from their despotism, though in the teaching of Christ we have the dignity and glory of the individual soul fully revealed.

I once heard such a fatalistic sermon by a Christian minister. He magnified the sovereignty of God until the part that man played in salvation was less than nothing, that is, it was antagonistic rather than coöperative. He justified his position by assuming that before the foundation of the world, some such scene as this occurred:—Let us imagine the council chamber of eternity to be M. Pasteur's office in Paris. The anteroom you find full of the victims of hydrophobia—they come from the four quarters of the globe—the peasant, bitten by the mad wolf in the wilds of Siberia, ladies from London snapped by their pets, victims of the vagrant cur sulking along street and highway, children from free America—men, women, children, huddled together, all fleeing from the same hideous nightmare, all starting in their beds at night choking and smothering with the same horrible thought! Pasteur enters, surveys the scene, and says, "I believe I will save only five of you. The rest can go, I might treat you if I would, but I choose not to do so. I will save these five for no special reason, except my own good pleasure, the rest of you need not say a word. My decree is fixed. I never change. You need not ask me to save you." And with slow step and backward-glancing eyes, with breaking and broken hearts, the sad procession files out—they are lost amid the turmoil of the world, sighing, groaning, raving, dying without hope! What a travesty on the name of God! Upon His love, justice, mercy—upon every attribute of divine nature! Perish the thought! I know not, nor want to know, such a God! No such God lives in the Bible. Plainly and clearly are we taught human responsibility—so plainly that there is no such thing as escaping it. For salvation is proclaimed universal and conditional. "Come unto me all ye that labor and are heavy laden and I will give you rest." "God so loved *the world*, that he gave his only begotten Son, that *whosoever* believeth should not perish." "God is no respecter of persons, but in every nation he that worketh righteousness is accepted of him." "He is the propitiation for our sins and not for our sins only but for the sins of the whole world." "Ask, and ye shall receive, knock and it shall be opened." "*Whosoever will*, let him take of the water of life freely." The invitation is world wide. Salvation is offered as a free gift. But it must be accepted to be efficacious. It will not be forced on any one. Compliance with this condition lies solely within the power of the human will.

The agnostic argument will not avail to relieve us of this responsibility. No man in a Christian land can say: "I do not know whether there is a God, or a Heaven or a Hell. I have no such knowledge and am therefore excused from any responsibility in the matter." Such ignorance does not excuse, because the means of positive knowledge is within grasp. For in John vii. 17, we find, "If *any man willeth* to do his will, he shall KNOW of the teaching whether it be of God." Here is the simple experimental test. Any man who wants to know, can know by making a practical test of religion, of Christ. God has thus pledged himself to give light to every soul that submits to His will and asks for light. I have never seen it fail. If it ever does fail, then the New Testament is a failure. I met a man in an after meeting one night who had not accepted the invitation to confess faith in Christ. I asked him why, and when pressed he replied, "Well, the truth is, I don't know whether there is any God. I have my doubts." I asked if he was willing to receive the light if God would give it. He said he was. I told him to take his Bible when he went home, read the Third Chapter of John, kneel and pray this simple prayer, "Lord, my will is thine, reveal thyself unto me, show me the truth, give me light!" He refused at first, but finally promised. That night he did as he promised, and the next evening he was the first man to leap to his feet to testify to his faith in Christ. I baptized him a few weeks later and he is now an earnest, consistent Christian. If you do not *know*, it is simply because you do not *want* to know!

Is it not true, then, as our text implies, that in the last analysis every man is alone personally responsible for his life and his character, the crystallization of life?

Could we make any other power responsible?

There are only three forces that operate on human life and character—the human will, or the creating and governing power within man, the force of circumstances or environment, and supernatural power, or God the Creator of all. If we could therefore shift responsibility upon environment or upon God, we easily escape. Let us see if it can be done.

1. Man is the creature of circumstances, does he not then cease to be a free agent? Hardly. For we must remember that truth is a bird with two wings. Clip either, and the bird comes down. It may be true that man is the creature of circumstances, but it is equally true that he is the master of circumstances.

I would not underestimate the part played by circumstance or environment in human life. This part is a most important one. The character of animals is largely determined by their habitat. The polar bear gives witness to the fact that the realm of everlasting snow has set its seal upon his hide and become a part of his very being. The Bengal tiger borrows his stripes from the variegated jungle in which he prowls. Climate, we know, has ever made its imprint on character, whether in animals or men. The philosopher understands this principle when he devotes himself to the study of Sociology, or the environment of man. So the Christian understands its value, when he comes out from among wicked companions and influences and unites himself with those who love God and truth and righteousness.

Yet this principle is after all a secondary one when applied to man. Man is distinguished from the mere animal by being responsible for the results of his habitat, or environment, on character; because he has the power to choose his own surroundings, to change his environment as often as he sees fit. If he does not change from that which is evil, when he has the power, he becomes solely responsible for the evil results that follow.

Besides, man has shown in the past that he can master circumstances if he will; that he can transform, make, and unmake his surroundings. To believe a thing impossible is to make it impossible, but when man chooses to eliminate the word "impossible" from his dictionary, he begins to work miracles. I remember the first time that I ever went through the mountains of North Carolina, the nearer I approached the higher and more impassable the Blue Ridge seemed to loom up before me, until at last the great dark cliff seemed to stand directly in the pathway and say, "Thus far shalt thou come, and no farther!" But pressing on and on, I found the turnpike gracefully wound around the cliff and passed out upon the other side. So do men make possible the impossible in everyday life, by simply saying, "I will!" and at the utterance of these words mountains become mole hills.

Men say they can't, when they can, if they will. In the war with Mexico a company of Texans were captured, and marched at double quick speed for twenty-four hours, and at the dawn of the second day they were nearly dead from fatigue and exhaustion, and could go no further, but when the order was issued to shoot all who dropped by the wayside, they started off at a lively gait and kept it up all day.

Alexander H. Stephens was a little paralytic —a life-long invalid. How could such a man achieve success in the rough and tumble arena of American politics? Yet he did. That big invalid's chair was a part of the Nation's furniture at Washington for a generation. Weak and feeble in body, racked with many an ache and pain, yet to the day of his death the crook of his finger was power. Men knew that back of the pale face, shrivelled hand, and dwarfed body that lay so lightly in that chair, there was caged the spirit of a lion, and all who knew him, loved, feared, or respected him. He mastered circumstances.

When Wm. Lloyd Garrison started his crusade against slavery, circumstances were all against him and his cause. He was hooted and hissed in Boston. His very life was threatened. Yet he simply said, "Here I take my stand. I will not extenuate. I will not excuse. I will not retreat one single inch—and I will be heard!" And he was *heard!* In the thunder of artillery that shook the world, he was heard! Amid the carnage of those four years of blood and death, he was heard! In the shout of four millions of slaves made freemen in a day he was heard! He made circumstances—made and unmade the men and measures of generations.

His physicians told Douglas Jerrold that he was dying. The old man started at the announcement, lifted himself on his elbow, and exclaimed, "What, man, *die* and leave these little ones helpless! I cannot. I *will* not die!" He lived three years longer. His indomitable will had grasped Death by the throat and hold him at arm's length three years. Upon the other hand we see the contrast in the man who did not bring his will to bear on circumstances, in a soldier who was sentenced to be shot. He was placed beside the open grave with the guard drawn up in front. The order was countermanded at the last moment, and blank cartridges substituted for the balls The guard fired, and to the surprise of all the man dropped dead. Not a paper wad even had touched him, but he died—because he thought he was dead. He had loosed his grip on his will power.

We can all remember times in our own lives when we stood face to face with some crisis, and realized with startling vividness our individual responsibility—realized it by an intuition swift and unerring, and that always stood confirmed by the sternest logic. I shall never forget such a time in my own life. It was in my early college days. I had begun to pin my faith to fate. I had my star. My heart was set on several prizes. Instead of hard work, I mused and dreamed and consulted the Sybilline books. All was propitious. Success was sure. I saw the new moon a hand's breadth above the eastern horizon unobscured by leaf or twig. The zephyrs whispered to the leaves and told of success—the stars all proclaimed it. Shall I ever forget that night in June, when with fallen crest, I walked out of the brilliantly lighted hall, with that awful decision of the judges ringing in my ears! I found that the stars had been talking about another man, and the zephyrs had whispered about another fellow entirely, and the moon had proven false to all her vows! I lay down on the grass beneath the kindly shadow of a spreading oak, and cooled off for an hour. That night all the idiocy of fate and fatalism, signs and wonders, oozed out of my body and passed off harmlessly into the earth. I had an interview with myself, took stock, and wound up with the resolution to work seventeen hours a day next year. I did, and was never afterward troubled with the moon, or the stars, or the zephyrs.

Even where man cannot change his environment, and when it is fixed, dark and cruel, he is yet master of the situation. He is endowed with a faculty by which he can transform darkness into light, and can make even the terror of his surroundings tributary to the glory of his character. The most wonderful bird in the Antilles is a little humming bird. He revels in those gleaming solitudes of tropical nature, where danger lurks on every side, among the most venomous insects, and among the most mournful plants whose very shade kills. He darts amid the foliage of the deadly manchineal tree and builds his nest among its poisonous boughs. He boldly crops and eats the fruits of this fearful tree, thrusts his long beak down into the depths of this venomous flower and draws forth the pigments with which he paints his crest the rich vermilion, and the sinister green with which he gives the metallic lustre to his triumphant wings, and from their burning poison acids derives his shrill cry and the everlasting agitation of his angry moments. What this bird does with poison, man has been able to do with poverty, jails, cruelty, persecution, and torture. As this bird transmutes poison into life and beauty, so man has taken the direst elements of life, and made character glorious therewith. Milton's blindness revealed to the world a Paradise Lost. A Bedford jail gave us Bunyan's Pilgrim's Progress!

Circumstances, then, have not mastered men when the human will has asserted its power.

II. God made man. Is not God then responsible for man's worthlessness? Hardly. God did make man, but man makes himself also. Character is all there is to man that is worth possessing, and God does not make man's character by any direct creative act. Character is the product of the human will. Will power God gave to man, and this is the instrument with which man makes himself.

It is useless and senseless to whine about the existence of evil. God does not permit evil. He cannot help it. Having endowed man with a free will, or the power of choice—there could be no alternative—evil was a necessity of this the highest possible creation from the divine hand. To have removed the possibility of evil would have been to destroy the power of choice, and hence, to have destroyed man. That is, he would have been simply a brute, or an automaton—not a man. Evil is, therefore, a necessary incident to the creation of man; and to charge God with the existence of evil is to charge him with the crime of creating man. Shadow is an incident of sunlight. We do not charge the sun with the responsibility of the shadow. Neither do we charge the existence of evil as a crime against the Godhead. This world would not be better, but infinitely worse without evil, since to remove evil would be to remove the possibility of good.

Good is the result of choice. A moral agent must be free. The very word *moral* carries with it the absolute necessity of freedom. This freedom is found in the power of choice. Will is the power of choice. Every will, therefore, is a perfect will. Choice is absolute. We either choose, or do not choose. He, who has not the power of choice, is not a man—he is deprived of the essential function of manhood, or moral agency. The words "strong" and "weak," therefore, cannot be correctly applied to will in its essence.

But could not God have made man so that he could not sin? Yes, God did make many animals incapable of sin, but we call them monkeys, horses, cows, and such like, not men. But could not God have so constructed man that sin would have been impossible? Yes, but he would have thus made good equally impossible. He might have prevented slander by creating man without a tongue, but such a man could not have sung songs in praise of his Creator. You can prevent a frolicsome boy from mischief by tying him hand and foot, but you cannot send him on an errand of mercy while thus tied—he is equally incapable of good.

The power, then, freely to do, or not to do that which is right, is essential to the existence of moral quality in any action. For God to have removed the possibility of evil would have been to destroy the power of choice, which is the distinguishing feature of free moral agency, or manhood. Let me repeat and emphasize this point. There can be no such thing as moral quality asserted of an action unless the power of choice was exercised by the agent.

To illustrate this: Some years ago a heavy passenger train was slowly puffing its way up the steeps of the Alleghanies. The great engine panted as if its strength were failing. The track was little more than a shelf cut in the rocks, with a cliff upon one side, and the precipice below. The scene was one of wondrous beauty, and while the passengers were enrapt with the sublime views that ever and anon burst upon them, suddenly the whistle of the engine uttered its sharp cry for down brakes. The brakesmen sprang to their posts and applied all their strength to obey the call. What had happened, or was about to happen, no one knew. With nervous questioning, people thrust their heads out the windows, or rushed to the platforms. The sharp eye of the engineer had seen an awful peril—a train of moving freight cars descending the mountain side upon his track! For a moment it was in plain sight dashing around a curve—no engine, no brakesmen, no sign of life. A collision seemed inevitable. The loss of life would be simply horrible! What should he do? He thought of a hundred things all in a moment, but none seemed practicable save one, and that he instantly decided to try. "Down brakes" he whistled. "Free the engine from the train!" he shouted to the fireman. In a moment it was done. "Now jump for your life!" The fireman leaped and scrambled to his feet again.

"Now fight the battle for us!" exclaimed the engineer as he opened the throttle valve and sprang from the steps. Freed from its load, the iron monster darted up the mountain side alone to meet the coming foe! A long gray streak of smoke marked the way as with the speed of the wind it dashed around curve and cliff and on to the mortal combat! Meanwhile down the track in full sight came the wild cars at a speed so fearful that, as they rounded the curves the wheels rose from the track and came down with a resounding crash. Then with a mighty tiger-like rage, they flew at each other! The crash shook the hills! A roaring cloud of steam burst into the air, and then the shattered cars, a grinding, crackling mass, rose higher, higher, higher until it quivered and tottered for a moment at its base, reeled and went thundering down the embankment in the ravine below. The grateful passengers draw near. There were the splintered ties, the deep ugly furrows in the road-bed, the broken rails and the nameless fragments of an utter wreck. The gallant engine was a hopeless ruin. There it lay like some noble wounded animal, with its iron ribs broken and crushed, its brass lungs burst, and its great heart torn out! It had fought a battle in which hundreds of lives and untold interests were at stake, and had won. It had died that men might live! And yet, that grateful throng never even inquired the name of the engine. They reared no monument to its memory there. And why? Because the engine had no power of choice. It was compelled to do what it did, hence no moral quality could be attributed to the deed, though similar in character to the supreme tragedy on Calvary itself! But with tears of joy and gratitude they blessed the *engineer* whose quick wit, daring plan, and instant execution had saved them from death. He was the hero of the hour—*because* he had the power *to do, or not to do*, what he did. We cannot, then, make God responsible for our sins or worthlessness.

The conclusion is overwhelming that upon every man's head rests his own blood. Men who profess a belief in fate, in destiny, who reach any success, always comply with all the conditions of the sternest success. Napoleon Bonaparte had his star, his fate, his destiny,— but he worked nineteen hours a day and slept five! He believed in fate—but he was fate! he believed in himself! Fate is the God of a fool!

Every thinking man recognizes that truth. Go with me a moment back into your life—down memory's halls. Let us turn aside into those secret chambers. You do not want to go in? Why not? If you are not responsible for any of it, it is all right. You could not help it! You hesitate; you know that in those rooms there are the ghosts of dead hopes, lost capacities, noble aspirations, and dark spirits flapping from out their condor wings invisible woe! You know that these walls are all hung with tapestry wrought by your own fingers; know, too, that the shuttle of no fool's fate ever shot athwart those tangled threads. You spun them, wove them, hung them—they are all your own!

No, God will not lasso you and drag you

into heaven. He will not bind you hand and foot against your will and carry you captive into the courts of glory! He lets down at your hands the rope of salvation by faith. He will not lash you to it by force. You must first seize it and swing off!

The law of the land, statutory and common, is above the individual. He is ruled by it, and cannot violate it—yet he has the right to dispose of himself and of his property as he pleases. He makes his will, and if the signature to that will is genuine, it becomes the law of the land, and the highest tribunal of justice cannot, dare not, set it aside! So do you in the royal chamber of your soul write your will, and dispose of an immortal soul and its immortal future. The law of God is above you, and rules you, but your *will* becomes the law of God! Heaven's highest court admits to probate that will unquestioned.

THE QUESTION OF HELL.

"The soul that sinneth it shall die."—Ez. XVIII. 20.

"And these shall go away into eternal punishment, but the righteous into eternal life."—MATT. XXV. 46.

SAYS a distinguished infidel: "I honestly believe that the doctrine of hell was born in the glittering eyes of snakes that run in frightful coils watching for their prey. I believe it was born in the yelping and howling and growling and snarling of wild beasts. I believe it was born in the grin of hyenas and in the malicious chatter of depraved apes. I despise it, I defy it, and I hate it." So do I, but the fact that I despise, defy, and hate it, has nothing to do with the bald question of its existence. The glittering eyes of snakes, the growling and snarling of wild beasts, the grin of hyenas and chatter of depraved apes, are horrible facts in nature; but the horror with which we regard them can in nowise blot out the facts; and it is simply childish nonsense to go into hysterics over the horrors, and think that thereby we may discredit the facts. I hate hell, and for that very reason must I be careful lest I underestimate its realities.

The religion that consists in a desperate attempt to escape hell and squeeze into heaven is a poor religion—so is the one that seeks to frighten folks into being good by a bloody picture of torment. Yet the religion that consists in wind and exclamation points on hell, and savage attacks on orthodoxy, offering the hungry human heart nothing in its stead, is poorer still, is infinitely meaner, is utterly contemptible!

I do not believe in Dante's Inferno—the Bible does not contain it; I do not believe necessarily in a hell of literal fire and brimstone, any more than I believe in a heaven that is a square walled city with gold brick pavements. The inspired writers exhausted the resources of human language in the effort to convey the idea of heaven's glory and of hell's woe. I may be all wrong in my conceptions of heaven, but its joy and glory will be none the less real for that reason. Orthodox conceptions of hell may be all more or less wrong, but its horror and misery will be none the less real for that reason. But the question as to the materialism of the future life has nothing to do with the discussion of the question in hand. The point of discussion now before us is a very simple one. Does Hell exist? There is an impression abroad in the minds of many that we have to-day a new theology that has annihilated hell. No graver mistake could be made. Unitarianism and Universalism maintain the existence of an awful hell. The so-called New Theology does not touch the question of its existence, but merely puts the query: " Will not those who have not heard the Gospel here, hear it after death and have another chance of escape?" It remains for an atheism that borders upon insanity alone to enter an absolute denial. And yet it is curious to note how many sensible people are tricked with such puny sentimentalism. Can such a denial be maintained for a moment within the bounds of human reason, to say nothing of revelation? It can not. We look about us and are confronted on every hand with facts that overwhelm us with the conviction of its reality. Appalled at its horror we walk round about this awful fact of eternity and try in vain to escape. It stands confirmed "by the nature of the mind of God, by the moral forces of the universe, by the prophetic menace of the human conscience, and by the analogies of all law." So that we are forced to believe that:

Hell is not a dogma, born in the imagination of cunning priests and used to terrorize childhood and coerce manhood into submission; not a dogma, but a necessity, the saddest, sternest necessity of the universe.

I. It is a necessity of Immortality. He who believes in the immortality of the soul must believe in hell. Whatever may be said as to the abstract question of immortality, it remains a fact that in spite of all doubts and fears we do believe in man's immortality. This belief is a part of us—woven and interwoven into the consciousness of personality itself, and is inseparable from our being, to say nothing of its confirmation in divine revelation. The human soul instinctively cries: "Believe in materialism if you will, but I am immortal, and my belief is as much higher and nobler than yours, as is the eagle, whose proud wing beats the air as he mounts toward the sun, higher than the toad that lives upon the vapors of a cellar."

Then, if you believe in immortality you must believe in hell. After death we must all go somewhere. We cannot all go to the same place. Certainly we cannot all go to heaven. To thousands, heaven would be worse than hell. I know some people who, when they reach the other shore and find no hell, would make one in short order. And if you put them off into a section of heaven, they would transform it into a hell upon arrival. The old story of the men in the wrong boat admirably illustrates this truth. They were rushing to the shore to catch their boats. One was chartered for a prize fight, the other for a Methodist camp-meeting excursion. As the whistles sounded the prize fighter rushed on the camp meeting boat, and the Methodist leaped on the deck among the prize-ring thugs. When they had started, the good brother with his Bible under his arm began to look for his friends, but could find only groups of profane, villainous-looking men, cursing, drinking, and playing cards. With tears he told the captain of his mistake and begged to be put off. It was a hell to him. The prize fighter wandered about the other boat and could find only groups of joyous men and women singing sweet songs, reading the Bible, and talking about religion. He sought in vain for something to drink, for congenial companionship. He, too, sought the captain, and, cursing the whole establishment, offered all the money he had to be put off anywhere—on a desert island—on a rock—anywhere that he might escape those songs and such companionship. It was a hell of torment to him.

Here is a man whose soul is going down, down, down, into deeper depths of infamy from day to day. He dies. Will his soul cease to descend and begin to ascend—yea, turn in its downward flight and leap into heaven? Can the stone dropped from the pinnacle, pause of itself in the descent, and, turning, remount to greater heights? Death is a mere physical incident. Can a physical incident work such a moral transformation? No, we say it is absurd. A mere physical change does not work a moral revolution. Souls, then, that are descending at death, are expected to continue that descent. Souls that are ascending at death may expect to rise to greater heights.

II. It is a necessity of Law. Philosophers, great and small, have ceased to maintain that this world was born of chance, or that it is run by chance. The spirit of the age bows before the universal reign of law. Law reigns supreme in the physical and moral worlds. Chaos no longer broods over Nature. We have come to make nature and law almost interchangeable terms. We realize that Nature acts with fearful uniformity. God and man may forgive, but Nature never. The name of Vengeance, of Nemesis, is Nature!

So must the moral universe be subject to

the reign of law. There is no such thing as law without penalty. Penalty is a part of the very definition of law itself. Law that is violated with impunity ceases to be law. Nature's laws violated wreck vengeance on the violator. Moral law wilfully and persistently violated must impose its penalty or cease to exist. That penalty is hell. If there is no hell there is no such thing as moral law, which no sane man can maintain. Is there no justice for the past? Has there been and will there be no adjustment of the wrongs of the ages? Will the dismantled cities, crumbled empires, enslaved nations, lost tribes, and dead races cry in vain for justice? Will the cry of the weak, of the oppressed, of the wronged, of the downtrodden, in the past, the present, the future, forever ascend and find no ear to hear, and no heart to pity? If chaos rules the moral world, yes,—if law, then a thousand times, no!

III. It is a necessity of Love. "God is love." It is curious to note the uses men have tried to make of this sublime revelation. There is a class of sentimentalists that play forever on this one string. They reject the plain teaching of the Bible on the punishment of the wicked. They seek to destroy all sensible theories of inspiration—in fact they absolutely reject the Bible, and yet in the next breath, proclaim a universal pardon for the race, because, "God is love!" Where did they learn that God is love? They did not learn it in their own souls, for an avenging conscience is there telling of righteousness and judgment. They did not learn it in the book of Nature. Nature is cruel and pitiless. That revelation can be found nowhere in the universe save within the lids of the Bible, and this Book of books they have spurned. Their hope of eternal life rests upon the sentence, "God is love," which can be found only in His Book, where alongside this declaration, the way of eternal life is marked out and made so plain that a wayfaring man, though a fool, need not err therein, and the penalty of hell hurled against those who wilfully reject this way.

Even an Ingersoll hopes! "In the night of death hope sees a star, and listening love hears the rustle of a wing," he says; and yet forgets that the star he sees is the Star of Bethlehem, and the rustle of the wing he hears, is the rustle of the angel's wing o'er the broken sepulchre!

God *is* love; but love is just. Justice is the foundation of love. Love that is unjust, ceases to be love and becomes a mere maudlin sentimentalism. The Bible does not teach that all who sin are to receive the same punishment—to be pitchforked into a burning cauldron and stirred up together. It teaches that some shall be beaten with few stripes, others with many, and that this punishment will vary in proportion to the light each has had.

The judge who loves his people and loves his country, must always be just. When Webster, the murderer of Parkman, was brought before Judge Shaw to be sentenced for his atrocious deed, he stood face to face with his old friend and schoolmate. The judge, as he gazed upon him, was overwhelmed by the memory of those years of companionship and love, and while the great tears rolled down his cheeks, he pronounced sentence of death. Was that sentence inconsistent with the highest love of humanity? Was it right, or wrong? If right, then it was sublime in its righteousness. If wrong, then it was infinitely damnable.

God is love, and because of this very fact there must be a hell. If God is love, those who know God, must know love; therefore those who do not love cannot go to God. They must go somewhere, and where they go is hell.

In East Boston a short time ago a man named Tom Rowland took his loaded revolver, went into his wife's room, and seized by the throat her whom he had promised to cherish, to tenderly care for, and love, and sent two bullets crashing through her bosom. As she lay at his feet upon the floor dying, weltering in her blood, the love of woman rose triumphant o'er the awful wrong, and looking up she feebly said: "Kneel down here, Tom, and let me tell you how I forgive you!" His only answer was to curse and kick her as she expired. He then turned and sent a bullet through his own brain and fell dead. Where did that infernal brute go? He died with curses lodged in his clinched teeth, with the scowl of hell upon his brow, with every drop of his foul blood boiling and hissing with eternal hate! God is Love. He was the incarnate fiend of Hate! where did he go?

I hate hell, but it is an awful fact. As a fact it confronts us. As a fact it must be met. If I could bridge hell with doubt I would gladly do it. I would rear a mountain where the chasm now yawns! I cannot understand all the dark mysteries of that world of woe. The traveller bends o'er the unspeaking precipice and drops a stone to sound its depths. He listens to hear the thud in the valley below. No sound returns. Only dead silence reigns. He drops another, and listens and hears only the throb of his own heart. So I approach this unspeaking precipice. I try in vain to sound its depths. There comes no response, save that in the deep of its black gloom I see written in letters of fire, woe! WOE!"

MIRACLES AND ROBERT ELSMERE.

THE PRESUMPTION AGAINST A MIRACLE.

If I do not the works of my Father, believe me not. But if I do them, though ye believe not me, believe the works.— JOHN x., 37, 38.

THE age in which we live is a stirring one. It is an age of stern questioning. All things are being cast into the crucible and tried by a fire seven times hotter than usual. I am glad of it. I am glad I live in this age. I like it. I rejoice in the widespread interest manifested in such a book as "Robert Elsmere." Out of such conflicts always come life and growth. I am not afraid Truth will suffer. Conflict only burnishes the shield and sharpens the sword of Truth, and she comes forth brighter and more radiant than ever. I do not nurse my creed as a tender babe, jealous of every wind. If my creed cannot take care of itself it will have to suffer, that is all. If I am wrong

I want to know it, and the sooner I know it the better.

The purpose of this book is to eliminate the supernatural from our religion, or, in other words, to destroy Christ in order to preserve Christianity.

The book is founded on a supposition that is not a fact, namely, that there is an overwhelming presumption against the possibility of a miracle, so overwhelming that the ordinary laws of evidence will not hold good to try the case. This is a purely gratuitous supposition and can be easily proven to be false.

A miracle is defined to be "an event or an occurrence which cannot be explained by any known law of nature; a deviation from the established laws of nature."

Is there, then, an overwhelming presumption against the possibility of a miracle?

1. Certainly the uniformity of nature cannot be legitimately used to prove that a miracle may not occur. It is very common now, however, to have this fallacy presented as an all-sufficient argument. In fact, this seems now to be the

principal stock in trade of our so-called scientific free-thinkers.

This is an old conflict, and the ground of battle has shifted with every age. Celsus, Porphyry, Julian, and Hierocles, the great infidels of the first three or four centuries, each attacked the miracles of Christ, but each on grounds so antagonistic as to destroy the force of their work as a whole. From Hierocles to Spinoza and Mill it was popular with the windy philosophers of that age to dogmatically assert that a miracle was impossible, and that, therefore, no amount of evidence could establish one. The philosophy of Spinoza and Mill placed a quietus on this sort of idiocy, and now our philosophic gymnasts are cutting somersaults over the continuity of natural law or the uniformity of nature.

The universal postulate of science is the assumption that nature will be found to be uniform. This postulate is the boundary line of the outermost horizon of the scientific world. Of that which does not conform to the known laws of nature, science can give no information, because outside of its realm. Science, then, as such, can never acknowledge a miracle, can never prove a miracle or disprove one. Science can only admit that, so far as the evidence goes, an event has happened which lies outside its province. The fact that the alleged miracle breaks the observed uniformity of nature could never destroy the grounds of its credibility, unless we maintain the absurd position that all the ultimate secrets of the universe are contained within the province of the now known laws of nature.

The uniformity of nature is merely an assumption based on a number of observations. If the miracle be true, then uniformity, in that far, could not be asserted.

Therefore, to plead the uniformity of nature against the possibility of a miracle is simply to beg the question. The issue is, "Was the uniformity broken?" To assert "No, it was not broken, because nature is observed to be uniform," is to walk forever in the lost man's circle, to come back each time to the place from which we started, and to prove or disprove nothing. For if the evidence establish the fact of the miracle, the alleged uniformity ceases to be a fact, and we must look for a new law or a higher law. It is an impossibility, therefore, that science can now raise an overwhelming presumption against the occurrence of a miracle.

It has become popular nowadays with a certain class of people to crown the scientist with a halo of infallibility, and to accept as an established fact that what he does not know is not worth knowing. I believe in science, I defer to it, I love it; but the realm of science is as yet a very small one, and man may know and does know many things that are not scientific. Within his province I acknowledge the right of the scientist to speak with authority. Here, say, is a man who devotes all his life to the study of the anatomy of a gnat. He has caught gnats, harnessed gnats, trained gnats. He has butchered gnats, dissected them, roasted, fried, and parboiled them. He has particularly and generally analyzed gnats. On the subject of gnats I agree at once that he is an authority, an expert gnatist. But he is not satisfied to stay within his domain. He longs to make wild generalizations from small premises. He leaps upon the lecture platform, strikes a dramatic attitude, and exclaims: "Behold! I see a gnat on yonder mountain, miles away!" This would not be so bad, but when he solemnly swears he cannot see the mountain, we beg here to draw the line!

Besides this, within his realm the scientist is still a man liable to be mistaken. Mr. Bobart, the director of a scientific garden at Oxford, it is said, found in the museum one day a dead rat. He took this rat, split its head, feet, and tail, drawing them in a peculiar way, and pressed and dried it. When in proper condition, he submitted it to a group of scientists for classification. They labored for days over the puzzling problem, and at length made their report, declaring the specimen to be a dragon! They wrote learned essays and even poems about this surviving example of a long-lost species. A rat! A cat would have known better. No, we cannot yet accept the dogma of scientific infallibility even within the limits of science proper.

But religion has no real quarrel with science over miracles. The scientist must believe in miracles, else the domain of science itself becomes a hopeless riddle. Indeed, so far from the scientist being able to eliminate miracles from the universe, he takes the student by the hand, leads him up face to face with a miracle, and leaves him there.

Even granting, for the sake of argument, that evolution is an established scientific fact, the working hypothesis of the theory of evolution involves three miracles.

First, the transformation of dead matter into life. Spontaneous generation is a bubble long since exploded. No respectable scientist holds that life spontaneously grew from death. Life comes only from life. Who supplied the first spark of life? No man has ever yet bridged the chasm that separates dead matter from live matter. The chasm yawns, as deep, as dark, as unfathomable as ever. From its infinite depths man has ever heard but one voice—the voice of Almighty God, Creator of Heaven and Earth! Here, then, is the great miracle of the ages. We know that dead matter has become live matter, and that some power "which cannot be explained by any known law of nature; a deviation from the established laws of nature," caused this transformation. Mr. Spencer and Mr. Huxley and all the hosts of science, lead us here and stand dumb before this miracle of miracles. "How did it happen?' cries the world. They reply in a whisper: "First Cause!" "Force!" They have renamed God, and call him "First Cause;" they have renamed the supernatural, and call it "Force." That is, they have reached the precipice, the outermost limits of the world of science. To make their own laws intelligible they must believe in a higher law, and yet they content themselves by juggling with words!

Again, the supposed transformation of the vegetable into the animal has never yet been explained. How the cabbage-head became a monkey is yet an unsolved riddle. "It cannot be explained by any known law of nature;" it certainly is "a deviation from the established laws of nature." Here, then, science leads us up to a second miracle, and the man who believes in the theory of evolution must accept it.

And then how the brute became a man is yet a mystery. How the monkey became a Shakespeare is an unsolved riddle. How the whining brute became the proud, erect, God-like man, with a heart that throbs with the joys and sorrows of ages, past, present, and future, "cannot be explained by any known law of nature." This consciousness of personality; this throbbing, immortal soul that yearns for the eternal and infinite, whence come they? Here, then, we are confronted by a third miracle. How, then, can science raise any presumption against the occurrence of a miracle, to say nothing of an overwhelming presumption against its possibility!

II. Every rational man is every day a witness to the occurrence of a miracle within the bounds of his own personal consciousness. Every sane man is conscious of the exercise of a free will.

The actions of a free will "cannot be explained by any known law of nature." They are "a deviation from all the known laws of nature." Science can never hope to reduce all phenomena to absolute unity, so long as a whole class of observed phenomena, mainly all those that belong to the action of the human will, are to be excluded from its postulate of invariable sequence. So far as science is concerned the human will is a miracle. Can science, therefore, prove that there is no such thing as will? The human will every day interferes with the law of nature's uniformity. If a human will can thus interfere with the law of uniformity, as every child knows that it does, is it not more than probable that behind some phenomena may lurk the interference of some other will higher than man's? In the human will, we are confronted with a fourth miracle.

III. The experience of millions of reliable witnesses testifies to the occurrence of another miracle, namely, the transformation of the natural man into the spiritual man—conversion. The conversion of a man from sin and selfishness to love and holiness, from the things he delighted in to those that he hated, is a mystery that "cannot be explained by any known law of nature." How the desperado is transformed into the saint we do not know, but we do know that the way in which it is done is "a deviation from the known laws of nature." Take the case of Rowdy Brown, as related by Dr. Pierson. He was one of the noted toughs of lower New York. He was a large, strong, bold fellow, who united the brutality of a savage with the ferocity of a wild beast. Passing a man who was seated on the forecastle of a Liverpool packet quietly reading his Bible, Brown, in pure malice, kicked him so violently in the mouth as to knock out his teeth; and this ruffian had killed men in California. Hearing of the conversion of one of his sailor-mates at the Water Street Mission, he swore that he would go down there, and if that fellow should get up to talk, he would force open his jaws and empty a bottle of whiskey down his throat. He went with his bottle. But there was a power there on whose resistance to his devilish plot he had not counted. While waiting for his time to come he became strangely moved himself; a new sensation, a violent trembling overmastered him. He could not even flee; the crowd was too dense, and his strength was gone. By the time his old chum was giving his testimony, Rowdy Brown was ready to faint; and when, at the close of the testimonies, inquirers were invited to come forward, he startled the whole company by dropping on his knees and crying, 'Pray for me!' The excitement was intense. He yelled and groaned for mercy, while his awakened conscience rocked and racked even his huge frame. Two nights of tempest passed before he heard the voice that speaks the soul into calm. But when he did get peace, he leaped from bed at midnight and roused the whole house with his shouts of praise. Rowdy Brown no sooner found Christ than he found work for Christ. In his intense passion to save men he would actually pick up bodily and carry some sailor to the mission and set down the astonished man on the anxious-seat, and then plead and pray with him till the heat of his own ardor and fervor melted him into submission to Christ.

Whence came this new power in the life of this desperado? The miracle of conversion alone explains it.

What else can explain the self-sacrifice and devotion of a thousand Christian lives you have known? We are told that a Greek architect was commissioned by a Roman emperor to build a great colosseum. He was told that success in the plans meant for him fame and fortune. The plans were perfected, the building erected, and the Emperor was charmed with the work. On the day of the grand opening the Emperor rose before the multitude and pronounced all honor upon the architect. To celebrate the occasion he ordered Christians to be brought forth from their prisons and fed to hungry lions and tigers. When the shouts over the bloody scene had died away, in one of the galleries the Greek architect arose and shouted until the vast assemblage heard: "I, too, am a Christian!" They seized him and threw him into the arena and his body was torn into shreds! There must have been a marvellous change somewhere in the character of that Greek—some power other than human must have lifted him from his seat of honor that day!

Yes, in the conversion of a soul we are face to face with a fifth miracle.

The facts in the case, then, are that experience testifies to a miracle every day for nearly 2,000 years in the conversion of a soul. Personal consciousness testifies to a miracle in the human will every day since the morning of creation, when man first said: "I will." Science leads us up to at least three miracles. A miracle, then, has certainly happened somewhere, and if a miracle has ever occurred anywhere it may occur everywhere. How, then, can there be any presumption against the possibility of a miracle?

MIRACLES AND ROBERT ELSMERE.

The Question of Evidence.

"I and the Father are one."—John, x. 30.

We have seen in the first examination of this subject that there is no overwhelming probability against the occurrence of a miracle. The ordinary laws of evidence, therefore, are all that we need to try the case. But the key argument which apparently overturns the faith of our hero is Wendover's new theory of testimony. His theory is that testimony is a science that has only reached a condition of order and credibility in modern times; that early witnesses being unacquainted with this science did not know how to testify scientifically, and, therefore, lied. That expert, or scientific testimony alone is to be believed. At first glance this theory may seem reasonable. At a second glance it is obviously absurd. At a third glance it becomes nothing short of a monstrosity. According to such a theory, Plutarch, Cæsar, Tacitus, Xenophon, and Herodotus, are not credible witnesses, because forsooth they did not live in our day. According to such a theory, we would crucify Xenophon and crown Zola, the modern apostle of putrefaction; we would outlaw Plutarch, and cannonize Ingersoll as a teacher of men! How utterly absurd! The truth is "expert" testimony may be the most utterly worthless testimony given in any court of justice, or inquiry. Put two experts on the witness stand representing different sides of the same case and ask them for information about the same thing. When they have finished, the court is usually overwhelmed by an impenetrable fog of lies. The simple man who does not know how to tell a lie, is the most credible witness. The author only saves Wendover, the character who advances this theory, from utter contempt by intimating that he is the product of a streak of hereditary insanity. And yet this theory, with insanity as its apology, is allowed to annihilate Elsmere's religion without a struggle.

The next main argument is likewise based on assumptions that cannot be established by the facts of history. We are told that the age in which Christ wrought was an age of miracles and wonders. That the air was teeming with them. That no great man appeared whose name was not surrounded by such a halo, and that the people held the simplest child-like faith in the supernatural. This is not true. The age was a superstitious one; but it was far from being an age of simple faith. It was, on the other hand, an age characterized by the decay of all faiths. The temples of Greece and Rome were deserted. "Stoicism had become a rock. Epicureanism was wallowing in filth." Infidelity, atheism, and scepticism were everywhere rampant. And o'er the crumbling ruins of the religions of the ancient worlds, Pilate peers into the face of Jesus and asks, "What is truth?" And did the air teem with miracles?" If so, why were none wrought in the childhood of Christ? If so, how could such a man as John the Baptist sweep like a cyclone over the country and yet it should be recorded of him by both friend and foe, "John wrought no miracles."

The question then arises, What is the evidence in hand? We have historic documents, whose genuineness is not questioned, which contain the direct testimony of Jesus Christ and His disciples to the fact of these miracles. We must accept this testimony, provided the remaining body of their testimony is found consistent with truth, and the character of the witnesses can stand the severest test. A witness stands or falls upon the whole of that to which he testifies, and that whole must always rest upon character for a foundation. Testimony that is thus consistent and harmonious as a whole, given by one whose character is unimpeachable, must be accepted as the truth by all fair-minded men.

Unity and *character*, therefore, are the two elements of credibility in personal testimony.

It requires no argument to prove that the body of Christian doctrine set forth by Christ in person and through His disciples is uniform and consistent. It stands confirmed by the testimony of more than eighteen centuries.

What, then, is to be said of the character of the witnesses? Let us take the central figure, Christ himself.

On examination we find the known facts in the life of Christ present us with a character of spotless purity and a personality absolutely unique; indeed the supreme miracle of history, a miracle that makes more than probable, yea, proves all the other miracles of the gospels.

I. All men, believers and unbelievers, unite in testifying to His goodness, to His perfection—that He was the highest and holiest, and noblest man this world ever saw.

II. He never worked or claimed to work a miracle for show. They were always wrought naturally in the course of His ministry. They were the natural outflow of the divine life within Him. They were prophetic and symbolic of a world's salvation, and were conceived and animated by the noblest purpose. He did not peep and mutter in the dark, use incantations, or jugglery. He unstopped the ears of the deaf, and the world turns to Him to hear the words of eternal life. He opens the eyes of the blind that man might not stumble; cures the sick, feeds the hungry for pity's sake; stills the sea to calm the fears of those who loved Him; raises the dead, that He may wipe the tears from the eyes of those who weep. These miracles were as clearly not the product of a superstitious age, as that modern jugglery and necromancy are not the product of the gospels.

He declared that He did these works by divine power. He declared that He was the fulfilment of prophecy and law—the promised Messiah.

He declared that He was God. "I and the Father are one." He spoke with authority and not as the scribes.

He was either insane, an impostor, or Jesus, the Christ, the Son of God, the Saviour of the world. No man has ever claimed that He was insane. Friend and foe agree that He was good, that He was upright, that He was the truest and noblest man who ever lived. If He was a true man, then He could not be an impostor. The conclusion is overwhelming, then, that He was what He claimed to be.

III. His character is a miracle that proves His claims, and He is Himself His own vindication. Think of it for a moment. All great men do suggest still with their greatness, narrow individuality. Watt suggests the inventor, Napoleon the warrior, Pitt the statesman; but Christ was the Son of man—the highest expression of the universal genius of humanity —this, too, in spite of His birth. The Greek has his national characteristics and weaknesses so the Roman, and the Carthaginian. The Jew was of all men most pronounced in his race prejudices and characteristics. The world has forgotten that Christ was a Jew. There was in Him the mysterious and perfect balance of severity and gentleness, of purity and yet the power to mingle with the impure. His purity was not of the human sort, for He attracted instead of repelling the impure. His magnanimity and self-denial were god-like. He first taught the world to love an enemy, and His sweet voice in the agonies of Calvary yet startles the world as He exclaims: "Father, forgive them, they know not what they do!" Such a character has never before or since belonged to mere man. He must have been more than man.

IV. History has established the truth of His claims; for the supernatural can be the only possible solution of the results that have followed His life and death. Circumstantial evidence thus adds its weight to an invincible personal testimony.

We remember that He was born of obscure parentage in a little village in Judea. He was born in poverty and obscurity, and was never given the advantages of an education. His ministry only lasted about three years, and He was crucified in disgrace at the age of thirty-three. And yet Mr. Lecky, the historian, testifies that the *love* mankind has borne Him has been one of the wonders of all generations. Yes, men have loved Him with a love so triumphant that they have walked bare-footed and blind-folded over burning ploughshares for His name's sake. They have gazed into the eyeballs of the fierce Numidian lion, and with joy exclaimed, " Lord I am wheat to be ground for thee!" They have died in crackling flames with songs of triumph and glory on their lips!

Lecky further testifies that this power has acted on all ages, nations, and temperaments, and has ever been the highest incentive to practical virtue known to the world; that it has marched victorious through the centuries of trial and struggle, and that the Church of Christ, when it has become degenerate and corrupt, has ever shown within itself the power of regeneration and new lfie.

Only thirty-three years did this obscure workingman from Nazareth live. His active period of work was only three years, and yet these three years are the pivot on which turns the history and destiny of the world. Reared in proverty and obscurity, with no rank or title, and no great man as His friend, hated, driven out and crucified in disgrace by His people—and yet He sways the world! The very calendar of time is His. The morning of creation is forgotten in the joy and glory of the day on which the shepherds heard the words, "Peace on earth, good-will toward men!" Kings baptize their children in His name. Cathedrals, poems in marble, rise to His honor and glory, while He receives the grateful homage of millions! The story of all the nations that have not heard His voice can be told in a footnote on a single page of history! The nations of the earth are His inheritance! How could these things be recorded of mere man? The only natural solution is the supernatural —yea, the only possible solution of such a life must be the supernatural.

V. Most convincing of all—He is now, to-day, the living Saviour for millions. Eighteen centuries have passed away. All personal mementoes of His life have perished long since. His birth place, Calvary, and the sepulchre we cannot find, and yet countless hosts to-day exclaim: "Whom having not seen we love!" He is the unseen presence that fills and thrills their lives with faith, hope, and love. During one of Napoleon's wars, a soldier was under the surgeon's knife. The blade was cutting near the heart, when the sufferer looked up and said: "If you cut a little deeper, surgeon, you will find the Emperor!" There are scores of men and women before me now, who so love Jesus, that if you should cut their hearts out, you would find Him there!

He is our refuge and strength, our hiding place in time of trouble and distress. Socrates, it is said, had a dream. He dreamed, that Plato as a young dove took refuge in his bosom among the folds of his tunic, until his wings were grown and feathers all full fledged. And then he rose, and soared away higher and higher, until lost in the azure blue of heaven! This dream has been the sweetest reality for those who have loved Christ. Thousands have sung "Jesus, lover of my soul, let me to Thy bosom fly!" In His bosom they have nestled till the storms of life have passed, and then on untiring wings have mounted to purer worlds on high!

As they have rested in His bosom, they have felt the caressing touch of His loving hand,

and there is no other touch like it! During the Civil War, there lay in one of the hospitals a young soldier, in a dangerous condition. In his delirium he called and called for his mother. She was summoned by telegraph. When she arrived the surgeon in charge said to her: "You cannot go in now, madam, the shock of your arrival I fear would be immediately fatal." So she stood at the doorway, watching and listening. She heard him groan, and with tears begged that she might go silently and take the place of the nurse by his side, promising not to speak or make herself known. She went. He lay with his face to the wall. He groaned again in pain, and the instincts of the loving mother overleaped all caution. She bent over and tenderly placed her hand on his fevered brow. Instantly he exclaimed with a sigh: "Oh, Nurse, how like my mother's touch was that!" We know Him because we have felt His touch, and no other hand is like His!

What think ye then of Christ? He is the supreme miracle of history. He authenticates Himself. The only natural and possible solution of His life and personality is the supernatural. You cannot separate His miracles from his personality, they are a part of Him, and He was the truth! There is, it seems to me, no middle ground. He was either a gigantic fraud, or the incarnation of truth. You *must* crown Him or crucify Him! His witness to miracles stands confirmed by His personal testimony, consistent, a unit, and based on a spotless character, and by the mystery of His personality (inexplicable unless divine) in its triumphant march through the centuries!

THE MYSTERY OF PAIN.

" My soul is weary of my life. . . . I will say unto God, . . . show me wherefore thou contendest with me?"—JOB x. 1, 2.

A YEAR or two ago a brutal murder was committed in a hotel in St. Louis. The murderer fled across the continent and put the Pacific Ocean between him and his deed. It seems that he all but escaped. He thought that he had escaped, but he had not. The strong arm of the law reached across the sea and dragged him back to justice—to a murderer's cell and a murderer's scaffold, and Maxwell paid with a broken neck the penalty of his sin. Sin and suffering, pain as penalty, terms so often linked together in human history! Law violated, vengeance and penalty follow as the necessary sequence.

That is a simple problem. It confronts you upon every hand. The child that tries to play with the blaze of fire, soon learns that it will not do. Nature's law violated always strikes back, be that law physical or moral. All that is necessary for a man to fully comprehend the fact is to simply open his eyes, and if he has any sense—certainly if he exercise reason, he must see it—and yet how many do not see it.

Now it is not to this phase of suffering we are brought by our study of Job; but we stand before the man of integrity who has suffered. And the book of Job, that tells this story, is perhaps the most unique piece of literature, sacred or profane, extant. Where is the scene founded? Some scholars say in Idumea; others say in the great Arabian Desert region, and still others fix it in Mesopotamia. It has no place. It was written for all places. When did Job live? What is the date of this book? Some say long before Abraham. Others maintain that it was after Abraham, and some say it was written by an inspired poet in Solomon's day. It has no time—no date—it was written peculiarly for all times. Who wrote it? One says Job wrote it, another says, Elihu was its author, and others say Moses, and some a poet of later years. It has no author save God, so far as human knowledge extends. No place, its locality the world; no date, its time, all times; its author, God! It stands forth in the dim twilight of human history, the dramatic revelation of the scene wherein God meets the creature and begins to instruct him in the first letters of the alphabet of life. The problem that confronted Job as he thus staggered beneath the providence of God is the problem before us.

What is, then, this higher mission of pain?

Passing by the innumerable inferences and lessons that have been drawn and truthfully drawn from the teachings of this book, we observe in perfect outline three answers to this vital question Job would ask of God. As the curtain rises and falls, and scene succeeds scene in rapid succession, we see the old patriarch *bewildered, enlightened,* and *crowned.* Or to slightly change the figure, we see him broken up, emptied, and then filled. We take it, therefore, that it must have been the purpose of God to thus bewilder, enlighten and crown, to thus break, empty, and fill.

I. We see him first bewildered. All his conceptions of life utterly broken—a complete wreck. Job's position had been one eminently satisfactory to himself. We see the picture of an ideal Eastern home. He had been a model man in many respects, upright and honorable, industrious and wise, and because of this had accumulated a vast fortune. We have every reason to believe that he was well satisfied with himself and began to feel that he had about mastered most of the ultimate secrets of life. He had reached the period of self-congratulation and satisfaction. His sons and daughters held their feasts in celebration of their prosperity every night, and over the revelry of each feast the old patriarch threw the mantle of a father's prayers.

But in the midst of these days of piety and prosperity, Job is suddenly stricken by a storm of adversity. In a single day all his property is swept away and his children killed. He still holds fast to his old faith, and comforts himself with the grim philosophy: "Naked came I out of my mother's womb, and naked shall I return thither: the Lord gave and the Lord hath taken away: blessed be the name of the Lord." But adversity touched him again. This time his body was prostrated, each nerve torn open and made the pathway on which the scorching feet of pain travelled to his inmost soul, and at last, all his old conceptions of life are utterly wrecked. In anguish he curses the day he was born and prays that it may be blotted from the calendar of time. In poverty and sickness, feeling that God and man were against him, he is led captive to despair.

He becomes a pessimist, and we cannot wonder that he does with the light he had. Viewed from a purely human point of view, the captivity of the world to sorrow is overwhelming to the mind of man. We seem to be captive to blind forces of unrelenting cruelty.

Nature around us smiles, threatens, curses, and commands, but never weeps. She rises in a thousand forms of beauty and sublimity and receives men's homage, but never stoops to sympathize with a sinning, stumbling child. She knows no sympathy. She has no ear for prayer, no heart to pity, no arm to save. She acts with fearful uniformity through laws as stern as fate, as inexorable as death, as merciless as hell.

The terror-stricken sailor climbs into the rigging of his doomed ship and cries in vain for mercy to the wind that shrieks in demoniac glee through the cordage about him. The wind does not care, the waves do not hear.

The victim who trembles in the grasp of an earthquake need not pray to mother earth, her only response is an open grave that yawns to be filled, while from the depths of her bowels comes the roar as of a hungry, maddened lion. The storm king in remorseless fury pauses not for cry, or groan, or tear, or prayer. The pestilence at whose subtle touch thousands fall, laughs at man's calamity. A single frost might stay the bloody work and bind again the blessed seals that held in manacles the monster's hands. The frost does not come. No! Mother's hearts lie still! More lives must yet be drained! And for many a morning still the rumble of that dreaded cart must be heard as at early dawn its driver cries, "Bring out your dead! Bring out your dead!" Nature does not care. Over all the bloody fields of our Civil War Nature never shed a tear. The grass grows only the richer for the blood that was shed. Nature only smiled the brighter from the nutriment of such rare food.

The sunlight steals through the window of the sick-room and lights it, but falls on the dung-heap with just as glad a smile, and plays on the burnished coffin lid of the dead with just as merry a twinkle. The sun does not care.

The water slowly rises along that fatal dam on the South Fork, higher, higher, higher, adding every inch ton on ton of pressure against man's weak masonry. Not one jot or tittle of her rights did Nature suspend. Every pound of hydraulic pressure to which she was entitled she remorselessly demanded, until at last with millions of tons gathered in her arms she leaped upon the puny structure, crushed it like a toy, and with the roar of a Niagara plunged down the mountain gorge on her wild mission of death! Shriek and groan rend the air! She does not heed, but lest any should escape, lights up the awful scene with conflagration piled upon the seething flood. No, nature did not care!

The view of the flight of woe through time is even more fearful. When we think that half the human race die in infancy; when we remember how delicately and exquisitely the human heart is strung to love, and that beside each one of those little graves two hearts have beat in anguish, and that this scene is repeated by unnumbered thousands with each wave of humanity that breaks on the shores of time, the thought is appalling! We hear the race through all the ages of the past, marching, tramp! tramp! tramp! to the music of sighs and tears! And the throb of that muffled music is overwhelming to the soul!

If this were all I know of human life, I would say too, with Job, Roll up the accursed scroll, seal it forever and hurl it into oblivion!

I will have none of it! But the heart of man has ever refused to be content with such a view, and in this bewilderment of despair the soul instinctively cries to God for light. So does Job. He seeks God's face. "Oh, that I knew where I might find Him, that I might come to His very seat."

II. In answer to this cry for light, God comes to enlighten. The process of enlightenment is first an emptying process. Job must be emptied of self and self-importance before there is room for God to come in. "Who is this that darkeneth counsel by words without knowledge?" says God. "Where wast thou when I laid the foundations of the earth? Who determined the measure thereof, if thou knowest? Or who stretched the line upon it? Whereupon were the foundations thereof fastened? Or who laid the corner stone thereof: when the morning stars sang together, and all the sons of God shouted for joy? Or who shut up the sea with doors, when it brake forth, as if it had issued out of the womb; when I made the cloud the garment thereof and thick darkness a swaddling band for it, and prescribed for it my decree, and set bars and doors, and said, Hitherto shalt thou come, and no further; and here shall thy proud waves be stayed?" We do not wonder that Job must exclaim in answer, "Behold, I am of small account!" This was important knowledge for the patriarch —knowledge in which he had hitherto been sadly deficient.

God now reveals to him a new meaning to life, and puts into his mouth a new prayer in harmony with that new view. Job had been a man of prayer; but of family prayer. His horizon was limited to his own acres, and broad though they were, his world was a very small one, and his prayer a weak and poor one —a prayer of about the import of our old man who prayed, "Lord bless me and my wife, my son John and his wife, we four and no more. Amen!" So Job had prayed for his sons and their wives and his daughters and sons-in-law. God instructed him now to pray for his friends, or more correctly speaking, his tormentors. Thereupon we are told, "And the Lord turned the captivity of Job when he prayed for his friends." The world was larger now than his own plantation, and his heart and life were larger because they saw a larger world.

There sits a broken-hearted mother beside her dead. She rocks herself to-and-fro, and talks about the little bright-faced girl that lies cold in death. She says it was all she had. She tells how the little thing had just begun to say "mamma" so sweetly, and through the big, hot tears she looks up and says. "Oh, what have I done that God should punish me so?" Nothing, perhaps, my sister. God may not be punishing you, but enlarging your heart, and giving to life a deeper, sweeter meaning. Your life was no larger than that cradle; there was but one child in the world for you; but now the world will be a much broader one and every little urchin you pass on the street corner will be kin to you!

III. We next see Job crowned. "And the Lord turned the captivity of Job when he prayed for his friends—AND GAVE HIM TWICE AS MUCH AS HE HAD BEFORE,"—"fourteen thousand sheep, and six thousand camels, and a thousand yoke of oxen, and a thousand she-asses."

Enlarged capacity is necessary to enlarged wealth. To receive a blessing there must be room. Any man is poor who lacks the capacity to receive wealth, and you cannot make him rich until you dig him out, and make room for it. There are some men you cannot make rich —they have no place to put it. There are many poor millionaires. You might give them the wealth of Crœsus—they would be poor still —and they would live a mean, and narrow, cold and selfish life. The Duke of Brunswick possessed his millions, but lived the life of a dog, in a miserable kennel he built, in which he dwelt, keeping watch day and night over his money and jewels. Says Jeffers: "He keeps his diamonds in a thick wall, his bed is placed against it, that no burglar may break in without killing, or at least waking him. He has but one window in his bed room, and the sash is of stoutest iron. A case of a dozen six barrelled revolvers, loaded, lies on a table within reach of his bed." Could any one be fool enough to think such a man is rich? The nameless cur that prowls through street and highway in search of bread is richer in all that makes life worth the having!

Why did not God give Job this great number of sheep and camels and oxen and asses in the beginning? He certainly had plenty. The Lord was not short of oxen or asses. He never has been—doubtless never will be. Why then did He not give them to Job? Simply because the patriarch had no capacity to receive so much wealth. He was too small a man. It was necessary for God to take the pick-axe of sorrow and dig out his heart! And when this was done, He poured in the greater blessing. We truly say that there is no full man who had not tasted sorrow's cup, for he who has known no sorrow is apt to be filled with the consciousness of his own good fortune and to have little room for anything else.

"Most wretched men are cradled into poetry by wrong,
They learn in suffering, what they teach in song."

So does God enlarge the capacities of the

individual and the nation sometimes. I love to think that God is thus to bless my own fair South-land. Out of the sorrow and anguish of the sad past, out of its darkness and gloom, out of its wreck and ruin, there is rising to-day a South richer and fairer than even the dream of the old! So that in tears of joy I can exclaim with Father Ryan:

> "Yes, give me the land of the wreck and the tomb.
> There's a grandeur in graves, there's a glory in gloom;
> For out of the gloom future brightness is born,
> As after the darkness looms the sunrise of morn!"

We see the light of a life apparently go out in the darkness of the night of sorrow, but on the morrow rise again brighter for every tear that has been shed. The shrub cut to the very root, will still put forth a fresher, rarer shoot on which will blossom flowers of sweeter perfume than the old. Even the Master was made "perfect through suffering" we are told, and so we can truly sing "In the *cross* of Christ we glory!"

So we must conclude that chance and accident do not rule the world, though a class of professed thinkers used to maintain that chance was the author of the world and its sole despot.

But when people examined that philosophy they found that it would be hard to run any sort of a world on that principle. Because if chance rules, the sun may rise to-morrow morning or it may not—altogether owing to whether it does or not. If a man jumps across the gutter he may land on the other side or he may go spinning and plunging through space till he strikes the moon. Horses may be born with one leg, or two legs, or maybe three, or possibly four. When this was all exploded, these same men began to cut somersaults over the eternal fixedness of nature, her unchanging laws—maintaining that everything outside of this is mere chance, that the good suffer and the evil likewise. But we learn here that God is looking on from the beginning to the end. Every motion made by Job is seen of God. Every breath that he breathes is noted, every word that he speaks heard. God walks near him, watches and listens, and at the proper time speaks His message.

We ought, therefore, to be better able to endure pain, knowing that God walks by our side. A surgeon had a dangerous operation to perform upon a child. He told the father: "I cannot perform the operation unless that boy's whole soul shall brace him up through it. You must explain it to him and get his full and free consent or he will die under the operation. The father went in and as best he could told the child and asked if he could endure it. With blanched face and trembling lips the little fellow looked up and replied: "Yes, Father, I can, if you will stand by me and hold my hand." And he did. And as the glittering steel, with caustic, sicking touch severed nerve, muscle, sinew, and flesh the brave little heart never faltered. So should you remember that a loving Father holds your hand in the darkest hour of woe, and that strength and health come out of the pain of that operation.

We learn, too, that God never strikes a child in anger, but always in love, and through the pain leads up to higher good. Such indeed is the universal symbolism of pain as expressed in various forms of the thought of the world, and in the work of nature, for through the agonies of maternity life is ushered into the world. When a common man is to be elevated to the dignity of knighthood, he receives three heavy strokes of the sword. Such is the thought that is interwoven in the rites, ceremonies, and initiatory observances of your various lodges, fraternities, and secret societies. This great truth is a real part of the higher and purer thought of the world to-day.

As I said in the beginning, I speak of the pain that falls upon the good as thus being educational. God does hate sin and does punish it here and hereafter by merciless pain. But I need not dwell upon this—you see it everywhere. Look into the judgment halls of sin, where God, man, and nature pronounce sentence upon the sinner. "Lazar-houses reeking with putrefaction and death, hospitals and asylums swarming with maniacs, whose cells echo with sigh, and shriek, and groan—dungeons, cages, and grated cells where guilt rots and raves, these, all these, and more, are but the feeble echoes of the truth 'Sin reigns unto Death!'"

But we have here the higher mission of pain. It is hard to understand it all sometimes—there is din and roar and confusion as we look about us, but we know that harmony is the great end. If you should go down town into one of the organ factories, you would hear the grating of ponderous machinery, the din and crash and roar of hammer and plane and saw, as out of the rude wood and steel and brass were being wrought the various pieces of the instrument. And after we think every thing is finished, there is still no music. Mr. Beecher, in describing the placing of the organ in Plymouth Church, says that when in its place, and you saw that every piece had been skilfully and carefully adjusted there was still no music, though every part was perfectly made, though every part was perfectly fitted. But the master of music comes with his tuning instrument, sounds his key-note and touches one of those pipes to see where it stands. Off it goes, howling and shrieking in the wrong direction, but he brings it down, down, until it rings in perfect harmony with his note. He touches another and that one goes howling and bellowing off at right angles from its true course, and back he brings that, until it breathes in solemn accord with the other. He touches another and that leaps off in the opposite direction screaming and shrieking in wild discord, and back, back, back, like a whipped child, he brings it. And so with every key. At last when all are tuned, and magic hands sweep those keys, there rises and swells the volume of music—sweet and rich and clear and full, until ceiling, wall, and floor, arch and cornice and moulding quiver and echo with its wondrous melody! So does God sometimes educate His child and so is He fashioning the world. Lord, help us, though with aching hearts and tear-dimmed eyes, to look up through the tears and see Thy smiling face!

PROGRESS.

"One thing I do, forgetting the things which are behind, and stretching forward to the things which are before, I press on toward the goal."—Phil. iii., 13.

Of all the Apostles, Paul attained the sublimest heights of Christian life. He had greater capacities to begin with, perhaps, and he bent all the energies of his great soul to the end to which he had consecrated himself. In this sentence he gives us the key that unlocks the secret of his success. He was the greatest of the apostles, and, therefore, this maxim of his life must be ever rich with meaning to the true believer. He counted not that he had ever attained perfection, but he was pressing on toward the goal. Do you aspire to noble attainments in Christian life? Then this inspired record will be pregnant with meaning for you.

I. The first principle enumerated here in

Paul's maxim of progress, is found in the first clause of the text, "ONE THING I DO."

Concentration of purpose is absolutely necessary to success here or anywhere. The man who would be successful in the races laid aside every weight that might beset him, and gave every energy of soul and body to the race on which he had entered.

The jack-of-all-trades is good at none. A man cannot serve God and Mammon. A man cannot have two masters. He must love or hate one of them. We cannot carry Christ in one hand, and the world, the flesh, and the devil in the other. The man who tries to sit down in two chairs at the same time, sits down on the floor. The man who gives two hours a week to the Lord, and six days and twenty-two hours to the service of the world or the devil, need not be surprised if he find himself growing worldly or even vicious. Success in any business or walk of life requires singleness of purpose.

The men who succeed are men of one idea. A young working man was one day bathing in the river Clyde. His eye caught the view of a beautiful hill overlooking the river valley. He thought what a grand thing it would be to have a home on that hill. He determined then and there to make that the one aim of his life. He did, and pressed eagerly forward in the race with his eye fixed on the goal. A magnificent residence now crowns that hill and overlooks the beautiful valley. The owner of the Clyde steamship line is the master of that mansion, the young working man of years ago.

A poor German boy once read of the siege of Troy, and determined to find the ruins of that ancient city that had perished 3,000 years ago. Through poverty and slavish toil he never forgot his vow. He procured books and learned seven languages. He became a merchant and made a fortune, and at last started eastward on his expedition. For long, long years he continued the search, and then startled the world with the great discovery. From the palace of the Trojan King, he brought treasures of gold, silver, and bronze, that had lain covered with sand for 3,000 years, and exhibited them to Europe. Scholars of all the world are debtors to Dr. Schliemann. Singleness of purpose was the secret of success. A fixed purpose we must have to master the ebbing and flowing tides of human life.

II. Oblivion of the past is the second principle of this maxim. "FORGETTING THE THINGS THAT ARE BEHIND." The racer who is striving for the mastery cannot afford to look back over his shoulder. He must leave the past behind. 1. Past blessings and achievements must be left. Paul's career had been a marvellous one—full of great achievements. He might with pardonable pride have contented himself with what he had done, and laid claim to the crown of sanctified perfection. Well might he have paused at this period of his life and reviewed the past. Doubtless the vision of the past did rise before him—the prisons through which he had gone, the uproar at Ephesus, the earthquake at Philippi, violence at Jerusalem, trials with the churches, chains at Cæsarea, shipwrecks, and stripes,—while before him passed the forms of Gallio, Felix, Festus, and Agrippa—yet he does not sit down and rake up the still glowing embers of so glorious a past, but even in old age turns his face toward the light of the future for strength and inspiration. Paul knew that Christianity is not a condition of passive bliss, but a throbbing life, and that self-satisfaction is the forerunner of stagnation and death.

Congratulation and self-satisfaction beget traditionalism, and traditionalism begets bigotry. The Pharisees were once the aggressive reformers of their age, but satisfied with their achievements they drifted into traditionalism and then into a bigotry that could imbue its hands in the blood of the Son of God without a blush or a tear. Such is the danger of blindly hugging the past. Of this is born that conservatism which seeks to limit the horizon of the human soul within the bounds of personal or ancestral experience, and has ever been one of the mightiest foes with which truth has been called to contend. It was so in Christ's day. Tradition was the most constant, the most persistent, the most dogged, the most utterly devilish opposition the Master encountered. It openly attacked Him on every hand, or silently repulsed His teachings. Even the Samaritan woman He finds armed with the ancestral bludgeon. "Art thou greater than our *father*, Jacob?" "*Our Fathers* worshipped in this mountain!" It was this spirit that nailed Him to the cross and mocked His anguish on Calvary's dark mount. It has ever been so in human history. Progress has always been made by a life and death and struggle with tradition and bigotry. It was tradition that in France held the *tiers état* by the throat, until the maddened giant in a fit of frenzy broke the grip and baptized the nation in blood. It was tradition that burned Bruno, stretched Galileo on the rack, danced a war dance around the fires of a thousand martyrs, and told William Cary, the apostle of modern missions, to sit down.

It is so to-day. The traditional ideas that dominate some of our churches form the greatest stumbling blocks in the way of aggressive Christianity. Why do we not make progress in the Lord's work as we should? Not because of ignorance—this is the most enlightened age the world ever saw. Not because of the increasing power of wickedness—the world is better than it ever was. Not because of aggressive infidelity—there is more faith to-day than ever, and the religion of Christ is just as comforting, just as sweet, just as strong as ever for the human heart. What, then, is the matter? Evidently there is a failure somewhere to adjust ourselves to the conditions and necessities of the life about us. "Can't we do this?" cries some wide-awake voice. "Well, hem! we never *have* done anything like that here!" says Tradition. That settles it, of course! What never has been, never will be, and what has been, will ever continue! How many churches have we to-day that are thus bed-ridden with ancestral rheumatism! The dear brethren sit down within the solemn walls, rake up the ashes of a once successful past, and shiver over it while the multitude without rush by the door, unmindful of its existence, laughing, joking, sinning, dying!

2. The mistakes and sins of the past are to

be left. Our mistakes we are to use, but not as millstones with which to drown ourselves. Napoleon was the most successful general who ever lived. It is said that he made more mistakes than any great general who ever lived. But his genius consisted in the rapidity with which he retrieved a mistake, and the certainty with which he avoided its repetition. The man who drops a glass bottle on the pavement would be considered a lunatic, if he should get down in the dirt, carefully collect the broken pieces, put them in his bosom, and hug them there until the jagged points should pierce and tear his flesh. Yet many a man does this in life every day.

You have sinned. Yes, I know, but you should not stumble over these sins, Christian friend, into others. God says, "I will cover your iniquity," "I will blot out your transgressions," "Go, and sin no more."

Peter sinned most grievously. He lied outrageously. He cursed and swore, and publicly denied the best friend he ever knew, his Lord and Master. But notice Christ's way of dealing with this sinner. Meeting the poor humiliated disciple after the resurrection, not a single harsh word does He utter, but asking three times for a declaration of his love—once for each denial—His command was, "Go now and feed my sheep." Put your feet upon those sins, and more humble and true for this deep experience, go forth to teach others! And what a glorious sermon Peter preached after that on the day of Pentecost!

Upon the other hand, Judas sinned, but no more grievously than Peter. The mistake he made was that he did not return to the injured Master and ask for pardon. He turned and looked in upon himself, and remorse overwhelmed him. There could have been no other result. Could Judas have turned his back upon his sin, and his face toward Calvary, and ascending that hill bowed at the foot of the cross and cried, "Master, forgive!" we must all believe that He who said to the thief by His side, "This day thou shalt be with me in Paradise;" that He who, gazing on His tormentors, exclaimed, "Father forgive them, they know not what they do!" would have said to Judas, "Go, child, in peace and tell a sinful world of my love for sinners!"

Paul had sinned grievously in his life. He had seen Stephen die, consenting to his death. He had kindled the fires of persecution throughout the land, devasted hundreds of homes and made a thousand hearts ache. But he did not allow his dark record to overshadow his life. He left that at the foot of the cross and pressed forward.

Shall we cower at the ghost of consistency? Shall the sinner, conscious of his sin, continue in the same path, because overwhelmed with that consciousness? I have sinned, and made many a sad blunder in my own life—shall I give up the fight? No! But putting my feet on those sins I shall use them as stepping stones on which to mount to a higher, purer life, and the knowledge of those dark hours I shall use as a club with which to beat out the brains of the Devil in future conflicts.

III. "STRETCHING FORWARD TO THE THINGS WHICH ARE BEFORE" is the third principle of our maxim. This is one of the distinguishing principles of Christianity. A lonely old prisoner is Paul—life all behind him, nothing before but death at the tyrant's hand. The world sees nothing to press forward to, yet he sees the invisible, and with eager footstep presses forward to the throb of unheard music, and the waving of unseen banners. Such is the power of faith, to make a desert blossom as a garden, and people the darkness of a dungeon with hosts of angels. So is the Christian thus in harmony with that higher universal language of creation—onward! The river murmurs it, the wind sighs it, the stars proclaim it in the temple of the heavens. Such is the spirit of the ages—the genius of the universe. These are the footprints of God, who walked with Enoch and has gone on before!

It is not only the privilege, but the duty of the Christian, then, to remember in the present that there is a future, and fix his eye upon it. It is the future, after all, that redeems the present from contempt.

I love to pause in the midst of the din and roar of sorrow, that comes from Nature's great tread-mill and listen to the music of a future, whose throbbing harmony will not be broken by shriek or groan, or sigh, or cry of despair! It gives me nerve to fight the battle of to-day. I look around me and see wrong triumphing over right, I hear the cry of the weak and the helpless as they are crushed by the strong, I walk amid the thousands who crowd our streets, and see written in their faces in great dark lines, sorrow and sin, poverty and misery, wretchedness and woe, while they jostle and crowd and trample each other to death. I love to think that the future holds another age with a life richer and purer, an age of peace and of righteousness.

Last summer I took an insurance policy to run until fifty years of age. The date of its maturity was 1914. What a strange date, I thought. What marvellous changes will be wrought in our civilization within those twenty-five years! And as the vision of that new world rose before me, I could but exclaim, "O God, that I may see the marvels of Thy salvation here wrought out!" I can endure the present with a glimpse of a sweeter future.

There are days in our individual experiences when we are to remember that there is a future. Sometimes one of those dark days will come, when the darkness of hell itself seems to settle all over life, and devils come with grin and leer to pound our aching bodies into an iron casket! Yes, we must eagerly press forward then. We must look up steadily at the clouds and by-and-by as they drift we will see a star. A great ship was crossing the sea and had been in clouds and darkness continuously for four days. The captain was out on deck anxiously watching to catch a glimpse of some heavenly body from which to take his reckoning. There was a rift in the cloud, a star gleamed through for a moment and then was lost again. But in that moment his quick eye had caught the bearing registered by that beam of light and he knew just where he was. He was lost before—now all was well. The star had disappeared behind the clouds, but he had taken his bearings and asked no more. He steered with unerring accuracy and reached his harbor. So in the darkest night if we look we are sure to see the gleam of a star that will give guidance to our lives, strength and assurance to our hearts.

Let nothing crush you, then, to-day—tune your ear to music unheard by common ears. You remember the Scotch lassie attached to a Highland regiment in India, who languished on a bed of sickness within the besieged fortress, where all were ready to perish from hunger and exhaustion. She was weak and feverish, but her ear was keen and heart hopeful. She startled them all on one gloomy day by rising on her elbow and exclaiming: "I hear 'em—they're a coomin'!" "Hear what, my child?" they said. "The bagpipes o'er the hills—they're a coomin'—they're a coomin'!" They told her no, that she was feverish and mistaken. But presently some one thought they heard, and then at last they all heard the music echoing o'er the distant hills and then the banners of the army could be seen, and salvation was at hand. Oh, for this gift that enables us to see the invisible and to hear the inaudible!

Friends, is your purpose in life fixed and single? Have you shaken off the spell of the past?

Are you pressing forward to that which is before?

Is the future full of hope, and do you eagerly press forward to it? Or do you approach it cringing, staggering, driven by the remorseless hand of time?

PLAYING THE FOOL, OR THE PROBLEM OF FOLLY.

"Behold I have played the fool."—1 Sam. 26-21.

How to keep men from playing the fool is a problem over which saints and sages have thought and wept in all ages. It is a great mistake to suppose that because we can boast of an intellect that our chief staple is intellect. One half of man at least is heart, one-fourth at least fool, and in the remaining fourth intellect plays a part of more or less prominence. This large streak of fool runs through the whole race, has been running since the days of Adam, and will doubtless continue yet for some time.

Diogenes found it in his day. It is said this quaint old philosopher was once earnestly discoursing on the beauties of virtue, and one by one his listeners began to desert him, whereupon he ceased his discourse and burst forth into a ribald song. The people hastened to return and soon a vast throng stood listening with open mouths. The philosopher turning upon them exclaimed: "Behold the assemblage of fools!" That same experience might be duplicated to-day on a much larger scale.

There are various degrees of folly, from the laughable foible to the highest crime. It is not of the innocent foible I wish to speak now. There goes the mild young dude, at whom people wink and smile as he passes. To his mind all the world runs to a centre, like the spokes of a wagon wheel, and he is that centre. People laugh, but then he is young and will grow, and so we pass such folly by.

But in the case of Saul we meet with a different species. Saul had no right to be a fool. Folly in him was no longer folly, but became crime. He was the Lord's anointed. He had been called from a humble sphere to wield the sceptre of an empire. Upon his shoulders rested the burden of a kingdom. He was the chosen leader and guide of hosts. So when we see him plunging into a career of domineering pride, conceit, and sin, there can be no excuse for such folly.

Let us make a brief study of Saul's career. How did he most conspicuously play the fool?

I. He made a fatal overestimate of his own strength. The first great victory Saul achieved seemed to have turned his head. Shortly after he was called to be king, as he was driving his herd home from the field, he received news that the Ammonites, under king Nahash, had laid siege to Jabesh-gilead, and that the people were in dire distress and implored his aid. Instantly he slew a yoke of oxen, hewed them in pieces, and sent this bloody war-token through all the tribes. Three hundred thousand of Israel and thirty thousand of Judah answered the summons, and assembling at Bezek, after a swift night's march they burst upon the Ammonites in the early morning and defeated them with enormous loss.

This victory rallied the nation around Saul as one man. But the consequence was that Saul became puffed up with the idea of his own greatness, and a short time after this we find him hiding among the caves around Gilgal with only a handful of half-hearted followers. God leaves him to himself, for He cannot use a man who is puffed up with the consciousness of his own power. Says Paul, "when I am weak then I am strong," because God's "strength is made perfect in weakness." Conscious weakness is the basis of the mightiest faith. Conscious power is a menace to all faith. Peter seeing Christ walk upon the water, walks also. But no sooner had the consciousness of this power filled his soul than he began to sink. I have no doubt that Peter as he began, elated at his success, exclaimed in heart, "Oh, ye weak disciples of little faith, observe *me* now!" He continued to sink until conscious of his own weakness he cried, "Lord, save or I perish!"

Conscious weakness is the frame of mind God chooses to use with greatest power. The channels are all empty then, and nothing interrupts the flow of divine force. Peter again conscious of his strength exclaims: "Others may leave thee, Master, but I will stand true unto death!" A little while afterward we see him in the court cursing and swearing and denying that he ever knew Jesus. But after those days of bitter weeping, in deepest humility, he hears the voice of Jesus, uttering no rebuke, but saying: "Go now and feed my sheep," and he went forth clothed in another strength than his own, and on the day of Pentecost, he preached the sermon under which three thousand were converted.

Knowledge of our weakness makes the Father above bend down in love and power. So does weakness rule strength. There sits upon my knee at evening time a laughing, bright-eyed boy. He is utterly weak and helpless so far as taking care of himself is concerned. He does not help me to make a living. He has always been a care and expense. But I love him, and the very weakness of his tiny little hand rules all the strength of my life! So do men rule God. The cry of the weak for help He always hears. The boasts of the strong in no wise appeal to His omnipotence.

Left thus to himself and fighting a losing war, Saul refuses to genuinely repent of his sins, and return to God's ways. He plunges still further into a career of monumental conceit that ends in madness and suicide. He thinks he can circumvent Providence. He thinks he can cheat almighty God. Samuel, the prophet had told him plainly that for his sins the crown should pass from his head to a stranger. But he refused to take this message from the Lord as final. He set himself about to remove David his successor, whom God had chosen and anointed. He mused after this fashion, doubtless: "I have sinned, I know, but I am not a common man, and I do not propose to reap the consequences of that sin. Men ordinarily do so reap, but I will not. I am a king, seated on the throne, a giant in physical strength, and I can remove this pigmy who dares to aspire to the throne. I was born under a lucky star and I shall not be thus snuffed out." In pursuit of this fool's resolve, on two occasions his life is spared by David, and at last he awakes to his true position, and gives utterance to the words of the text, which form a fitting epitaph for his tomb.

Alas, the world to-day is full of such fools—men who think they can cheat God; that they can sow tares and reap wheat; that they can sow nightshade and reap morning-glories. They know that other men have failed, but then they are cunning, shrewd, brilliant fellows. They were born under lucky stars. They always were lucky. And so they think to lead a double life, and cheat God and the world. Outwardly they will have a whitewash coat of morality, but deep beneath the surface their heart's blood will circulate. There every nerve shall tingle with life's sweetest forbidden pleasures. There they shall really *live*—a life deep and capacious, of license and licentiousness! The pathway of human life is literally strewn with the skeletons of such fools, and still the myriad hosts rush on where these have fallen!

See the devotees of lust as they crowd to that door around whose steps bleach the bones of thousands! They heed it not. On they go to a fool's grave, while thousands more crowd to take their places. The crown prince of an empire in our own time tried this game of double play. What had he to fear? Wealthy, petted, the heir to a throne; and yet this man died the other day in shame and disgrace, died the death of a miserable dog. Rudolph, Crown Prince of Austria, was his name. I do not marvel that Austria mourns in sackcloth and ashes! Men must sow what they reap.

The man who begins his career of drink enters the broad highway on either side of which have been dumped the reeking bodies of the dead until the road lies twixt two mountains of putrid clay, and the awful stench breeds pestilence for a nation! And still on they go, cursing, crowding, jostling each other for precedence in the lines that press on to death and hell!

There goes a young man into a gambling den—food for sharks! He has heard of the danger; yes, but he is a "lucky boy." He was born when the signs were right, he says. A young fly sails around the room and sees a spider's web. He pauses to examine. "Why," says he, "there is nothing very dangerous about this! There seem to be handsome, nicely-carpeted apartments in there. I have heard much of the danger, but I don't see it. I've even heard an old green-bottle fly describe it with terror—but my opinion is that he was a coward. I believe I'll go in!" He goes in. There is a faint little buzz, and then you see his legs and wings pitched out the door, while the spider merely picks his teeth, crosses his legs, and waits for the next fool.

A young rabbit hopped into a garden one day in which a nice bed of cabbage was neatly inclosed in a wire net. He looked at the cabbage and he looked at the net. He had heard of the danger of traps and nets, but this did not look dangerous—especially when he caught sight of the luscious cabbage within. So he slipped inside and began to eat. The more he ate the better he liked it. He stayed all night. He ate cabbage all next day, and smacked his lips and wondered what a dunce he had been not to have eaten cabbage before. He stayed all week—two weeks—three weeks—and then thought he would run back to the old place and see how things looked. But when he went to go out he found that he had grown to be a large-sized rabbit and that the hole he came in at had not grown any. So he did not get out. The owner of the garden came in that day, saw him, seized him by the neck, took him to the kitchen, and chopped his head off.

Such is the end of a fool.

"Be not deceived, God is not mocked,"—literally, you cannot turn up your nose at God—"whatsoever a man soweth that shall he also reap."

II. The folly of Saul was conspicuous too in the fact that he always failed in the proper exercise of foresight—he seemed to use only what might be called his "hind-sight." The text gives a fair sample of his conduct. He says, "Behold, I *have* played the fool!" He never seemed to be able to grasp the idea that he was about to play the fool and stop in time. His philosophy was always retrospective. It is said that there is a race of people gifted only with "hind-sight," and that when they want to go forward they must turn around and go backward. Saul seems to have been the forerunner of this race.

What a sad thing it is that men can be brought to see their folly only by looking backward after some tragic exhibition of it. Such are the men who put off repentance to their death bed, the hour most utterly unfit for repentance, of all the hours of life from the moment of birth to the expiring gasp. The saddest sight I ever saw was a man trying to repent on a death bed! I pray to be spared many such sights. All in confusion—the physicians there, the loved ones weeping in terror, angels and devils hovering near, eternal life or death quivering in the balance—oh! infinite fool, such a man!

Such is the man who neglects his pet sin until it has mastered and crushed him. It is said an Englishman once took a young tiger from the jungles of India to his home in London and raised it as a pet. It grew rapidly, and the big brindle thing followed him about the streets to the terror of all who saw him. People remonstrated with him, telling him of the danger to himself and others. He replied, "Oh, there is no danger, I have raised him from a little cub. He has never tasted blood, and so is as gentle as a cat." One day the master fell asleep on the lounge and the pet sat by licking his hand. The tongue of the tiger is like the teeth of a file, and as the tongue passed rapidly over the hand at last the outer skin was broken, and then each stroke came nearer and nearer to the blood until a little blood-vessel was broken and a few drops of blood were lapped upon the tongue of the brute. Instantly all the fires of his wild nature were kindled, and in a moment the pet was transformed into the wild beast of the Indian forest. Leaping back and crouching close to the floor, his great eyes glowing like balls of fire, his tail waving slowly to and fro, he prepared to spring upon the throat of his victim. At this moment, strangely enough, the man woke, and realizing his awful danger, silently drew his revolver and sent a bullet through the vitals of the tiger. He barely escaped with his life, and more than once reflected on his stupendous folly. So do men nurse their pet sins until destroyed by them! Saul was preëminent in such folly. He never saw a hole until he fell in it. He never saw a ditch until he was up to his chin in it. He never saw a precipice until a mangled heap at the bottom he turned to see from whence he had fallen. And the generation of Saul is not yet extinct.

Such a man was he who toiled a lifetime and won a fortune, and putting his fortune all into an enormous diamond, belted it about his body and sailed for his native land. On board the ship he exhibited his diamond in season and out of season. He was wont to amuse himself by tossing it high up in the air and catching it, while the gaping crowd looked on in wonder at his audacious folly. They begged him to stop, but he persisted the more. He drew near the ship's edge with it and in pure wantonness tossed it up there. Higher and higher he threw it, each time catching it with perfect accuracy. Higher than ever he threw it and caught it. Again he threw it, when, *lurch!* went the great ship to one side, and down into the depths of the sea like a loosed beam of light darted the precious stone! With pale cheeks and choking heart back from the bulwarks the fool staggered a miserable pauper! So I see men stand on the edge of a precipice and in pure wantonness toss up their immortal soul, gambling with the devil! As the precious treasure flashes through the sunlight of God's word, its pure quality and enormous value are revealed. Dying men and women, why should you be guilty of such madness!

Such are they who utter those sad words, "It might have been!" Such are they who exclaim, "O God, roll back thy universe and give me yesterday!" And the only answer that returns is the sad echo of their own wailing voice!

WHAT IS LOVE?

"This is the love of God, that we keep his commandments."
1 John, 5–3.

THE grandest conception of deity ever attained by heathen mind perhaps was the Phidian Jupiter. It was wrought of ivory and gold, a carved figure, seated upon a throne with majestic air, holding in its left hand a statue of victory and in its right the sceptre of empire. Says a great preacher in describing it: "So vast was this extraordinary work, that sitting in the chair of state, it towered forty feet in height. Into no other figure and face had art ever thrown such astonishing majesty. Men made pilgrimages to see it, and he was counted unfortunate who died without seeing the Phidian Jupiter. And when on festival days the priests drew back the purple curtain, the vast statue, white as snow and yellow as gold, shone forth with such amazing lustre that the crowd were subdued to tears." And yet no heart throbbed there. No light flashed in those eyes. Great as was this conception, it was far below the Hebrew's idea of God. "In no carved stone, ivory or gold did he ever seek to express the majesty of Jehovah. The morning light was but the golden fringe of his garments. His slightest look they called the lightning. His lowest tones were the sonorous bolts of the resounding storms."

Greater still than all these conceptions, is the simple declaration of the New Testament, "God is love!"

And yet within the scope of this magnificent conception, within this vast empire of infinite love, we poor mortals somehow lose our way at times. We embrace curious definitions of love, especially of our love toward God. Rejoicing in the liberty of love we too often bound into the license of mere sentimentalism. Let us listen for a moment to John, the great apostle of love, who leaned his head on the Saviour's breast and drew the veil from the secrets of his inmost heart. We live in an era of preaching when it is popular to exhalt love. I rejoice in that fact. But let us be sure we understand what love is.

"This is the love of God, that we keep his commandments."

I. Love, then, is no mere blissfulness of feeling. It is oneness of will with the beloved.

Says Christ, "If a man love me, he will keep my words." "He that hath my commandments and keepeth them, he it is that loveth me." Two people cannot love each other whose wills clash. The conflict of will precludes the beginnings of love, and will destroy love that is begun. Two people whose wills forever clash cannot live together in peace.

But love not only agrees with the expressed will of the beloved, that is, it not only obeys the commands, but runs before, and hastens to anticipate the desires of the loved one. Says the true husband, "What would please her; what can I do for her; what can I give her that will make her heart beat with greatest joy?"

II. Obedience, then, is the sure evidence of love. "Hereby do we know that we know him, if we keep his commandments. He that saith I know him, and keepeth not his commandments, is a liar and the truth is not in him. But whoso keepeth his word, in him verily is the love of God perfected; hereby know we, that we are in him. He that saith he abideth in him ought also to walk as he walked."

We know that the patriot loves his country because he obeys his country's call. When the bugle's shrill cry called him to do and die for the flag, he came, and when the command was given to charge, he walked over dead men's bodies and on into the very jaws of death. The man who says, "I love my country" and yet refuses to obey his country's call, lies.

The child who says, "I love my mother!" and yet with a wilful toss of the head refuses to obey that mother's voice, does not love. He who says "I love God," and yet refuses, or neglects to obey his simplest commands, deceives himself. He does not know what love is. Obedience always accompanies and is the evidence of love. "This is the love of God that we keep his commandments."

Do you love Christ? If so, two commands you will hasten to obey—to confess that love and to follow Him. "Every one, therefore, who shall confess me before men, him will I confess before my Father." "With the heart man believeth unto righteousness and with the mouth confession is made unto salvation." If a man love Christ he will "deny himself, take up his cross and follow." There are some people who are trying to squeeze into heaven doing just as little as they possibly can. They are never baptized because they think they can squeeze in without it. "The thief on the cross was not baptized," they say. They are well up on the thief on the cross and lug in that solitary example of such a salvation in season and out of season. But alas, they forget that he was a dying thief—they are living thieves. He stole from men—they try to rob God, and the difference is one of infinite importance.

The law of agency holds the agent responsible not only for what he does, but also for what he might do. So does God who has intrusted to our care the priceless value of an immortal soul. He holds no man responsible for that which is impossible; He holds us accountable only for what we can do, but up to the full measure of possibility.

Let no one deceive himself. Ecstatic emotion is not religion. We must not lay too much stress upon "feeling." Feelings are unreliable. Sad indeed must be the Christian life of him whose faith rises and falls with the fluctuations of his feelings. Mere feeling is affected by a thousand things, that have nought to do with true religion. The weather may be the cause of joyous or sad feelings. I heard the son of a cobbler in my native village give his Christian experience. In his description of his conversion the preacher asked him: "Well, Peter, how did you feel?" He replied, "I felt right soft!" He did feel a little soft, and that was all there was to it. He did not hold out. Religion does not consist in "feeling soft." Obedience is the evidence of love.

Let the creed crank be not deceived. He may be orthodox and yet be lost. He may hold the five points of Calvinism and yet go to hell. A man may know the Bible so well that he could thrust a pin through its leaves and tell you what word on each page was punctured by it and yet know nothing of saving faith. The devils believe. It is not what a man believes or knows with his brain that saves. It is what he believes with his heart. "With the heart man believeth unto righteousness." "Under whose preaching were you converted," was asked of an applicant for baptism. "Under nobody's preaching," he replied. "Under my mother's practising!" No questions need be asked about the genuineness of her religion.

"I love God and my neighbor, and this is the fulfilment of all the law," says a man. If he does love God with all his soul and his neighbor as himself he surely will be saved. But he must not forget that love toward God implies implicit obedience to His commands. Have these commands been obeyed? Has he accepted Christ? Is he walking in obedience to His commands? If not, then his love is a mere hollow pretence. "This is the love of God, that we keep his commandments." Pharnaces while still a rebel sent a diadem to Cæsar. Cæsar, declining, sent the reply, "Your obedience first, and then your gifts." A man in open rebellion against God need make no pretensions to love.

The hypocrisy of the man who cries, "I am a philanthropist, but I'm opposed to hospitals!" is only too patent.

What would you think of the man who cries: "I love my country, but I can't give any of my time to it, and cannot afford to expose myself for the flag—some other man must do that! Whenever there is a love-feast, count me in, but if there is a fight, I have an engagement elsewhere." Such a patriot would be beneath the contempt of a respectable dog who claimed any attachment for his native heath.

Love always, then, manifests itself in oneness of will and obedience. Blissfulness of feeling, morbid emotion, and extravagant language, may be the effervescence of a fervid love, but they give no assurance of its existence, for they can flow just as violently from a weak sentimentalism. The case of Lord Bulwer bears witness to this. His so-called love letters to Lady Bulwer attain the climax of idiocy. Thus begins and ends one of these letters: "My Dearest and Kindest And Most Bootiful Poodle:—Me went down to the House of Lords, etc.

"Good-by, my darling, my angel, my life, my Poodle,

Oo own Puppy."

Do you wonder that a few years after marriage that man was found rushing upon his wife with a carving knife? As he sprang toward her with the drawn blade she exclaimed, "For God's sake, Edward, take care what you are about!" Whereat he dropped the knife, and with the ferocity of a tiger sprang upon her and bit a hole in her cheek.

No, love is not mere blissfulness of feeling. This is the love of God that our wills be one with His, that we keep His commandments.

THE TEMPERANCE PROBLEM.

Within the memory of a generation marvellous progress has been made in temperance work. The moral tone of the community has been lifted to mountain heights as compared with the status of forty years ago. Scarcely longer ago than that, in one of the old thirteen States, at a social gathering of Baptist preachers, it is said that the brethren imbibed so freely that it was impossible to close the evening's deliberation with prayer. In an adjoining State about the same time, at a Methodist Conference, a resolution was introduced to the effect that it was the opinion of the conference that a minister should not be allowed to sell ardent spirits. The resolution was voted down by an overwhelming majority. What a contrast with the present attitude of these churches!

In view of the progress that has been made,

there is only hope and inspiration in the future. I believe that twenty-five years from to-day there will not be an open legalized saloon on American soil from the frozen seas of Alaska to the orange groves of Florida, from Maine to the Rio Grande, and from sea to sea!

But the time has passed for mere sentiment on the subject, for doggerel poetry and lofty abstractions. The hour demands action—persistent, systematic, remorseless, aggressive, along all lines, *religious, social,* and *legal.* For with all our progress, the total consumption of alcoholic liquors has yet increased. Between the forces of civilization and the forces of intemperance there is an irrepressible conflict. They cannot both survive the struggle of another quarter of a century. One must go down.

I. The hour demands action along religious lines. The temperance movement of this age is a religious movement, and the principles that underlie it are the fundamental principles of Christianity. Men have said the church has nothing to do with this question. If a giant evil can grow up thus in our midst, slaying its thousands and tens of thousands, laying its impious hands with debauching touch on the ballot and the legislator, hurling defiance in the face of society and the church, crushing the hearts and homes of the weak and helpless,—if the church has nothing to do with all this in God's name, what are we here for?

Every church should be in itself a great temperance organization, whose pastor gives forth no uncertain sound on the subject. This day is rapidly approaching. The minister of the gospel who does not now preach temperance is a rare bird, and he is getting rarer. You see him only now and then. You see him seated on the bare limb of some dead tree, chattering about the good old times of the dark ages. He will soon be so rare that you will find him only in the cage of a dime museum. God speed the day!

There are still a few good brethren, too, who have fallen behind the procession, because they have pinned themselves to some crotchet or other, and out of pure stubbornness, or fear of inconsistency, do not investigate and turn. It may be a little embarrassing, but, brother, it is better to change if you are wrong. To all such I would commend for study the sincerity of Brother Franks of North Carolina. It is said that he went into the pulpit of his country church one day, and in the midst of his services discovered that he had put on his stockings wrong side out. He at once paused, and began to take off his shoes to put things right. A brother sitting by said:

"Brother Franks, don't pull off your shoes here before the congregation!"

"Yes, I will," replied Brother Franks;" whenever I find that I am wrong, *then* and *there* I turn." And he turned! After all, if vitally wrong, is it not better to turn, even if it is somewhat embarrassing?

II. The hour demands action along social lines. The temperance movement is likewise a lofty social movement. In our intense fight against the thing, we must not lose sight of the principle of the thing. The foundation of successful temperance reform is educational. It is time that we fixed on a firm basis in our social relations, the truth that intemperance is not a jolly weakness, or a phyiscal disease, but a *crime*. We have passed the period of apologetics, and are in the realm of eternal axioms.

Drunkenness is pronounced a crime by the law of God. " No drunkard shall inherit " thunders His Word! It is pronounced a crime by the science of medicine. Attempts to treat drunkenness as a physical disease have been conspicuous only as failures.

It is pronounced a crime by the civil law. Divorce is granted for this cause upon the theory of criminality. Drunkenness cannot be pleaded in a court of justice in explanation or extenuation of any crime, because one crime cannot be pleaded in justification of another. So is the man arrested who is found drunk upon the streets.

This law, written by the hand of God and echoed by science and civil law, must be translated into our social vernacular. Woman, the reigning sovereign of polite society, can have much to do with this work. It should be enforced in the parlor and the dining room. Especially should it be enforced at the marriage altar. Would you marry a criminal, my dear young girl? She shudders at the idea. But if a man who gets drunk comes along and is good looking, she marries him to reform him! O climax of idiocy! Yes, there he goes. He was kicked out of a dry-goods store. The proprietor came to him one morning after a debauch, and said: "Young man, this is a business establishment. We have no room for such cattle as you here. There is the door!" He was employed by a railroad company, but on discovering his habits, they kicked him out there. The conductor of a street car kicked him off and would not let him ride. Kicked out of business, kicked off the public highway, kicked out everywhere—but about this time some girl who never saw him before, and not akin to him, opens her arms and says: "Come to my arms, my own stricken dear!" And he comes! He always comes. He has been waiting to come for some time. In the ecstasies of mere moonshine sentiment she exclaims: "O darling, I could live with you on bread and water!" And he chimes in, "me too!"—but with the mental reservation that if she can furnish the bread, he will shuffle around and try to get up a little water! Then they join hands and down, down, down to a hell of poverty and woe side by side they go! Oh, the pity of it!

We should teach the young to shun the cup as they would shun arsenic or strychnine. We should teach them the awful danger of the drink habit and the drink appetite. But it seems to me care should be taken lest we overdo the idea of appetite. There are very few people who acquire an appetite from one drink. Appetite is not the result of the first drink, but of the five hundredth rather. It is the result of unrebuked and unpunished persistence in the crime of intemperance. We should teach a lofty contempt for drinkers and drinking. I have seen young men who made great pretensions to the ravages of an insatiate appetite for alcohol, who simply lied in such pretensions. They drink as an excuse for utter worthlessness, while the world pathetically attributes it all to appetite. Without hereditary taint the human stomach will never cry for the infernal stuff until you first soak and rub it in the sewer.

I shall never forget my first drink. I was sea sick for the first time. I had retired to my stateroom and was wrestling with the enemy. My friend with a remedy called and advised. He said the thing to do was to go down to the bar and get a cocktail. At first I declined. Finally, I decided to go. With as much dignity as I could summon, for I did not want to appear green, I walked up to the bar and called for a cocktail. The barkeeper stared at me and asked: "Gin, or whiskey?" This was a problem I had never met before, I did not know it was made two ways. I pondered. It seemed to me that "whiskey" sounded very raw and vigorous, vulgar and formidable, while "gin" sounded short and simple and upon the whole struck me as the much milder term. I told him to make it gin. He made it gin. I took it. I do not remember everything that immediately followed, but as I look back now, it seemed to me that I had swallowed a glass of red-hot molten cast iron. And when it struck bottom it seemed to crystallize in the shape of a steam saw-mill with a circular buzz saw making a thousand revolutions a minute! I did my best, but I could not hold it down sixty seconds! I have heard of people eating fish-hooks and axe-handles, chewing matches and scrap-iron; and as for me you may give me fish-hooks and axe-handles for breakfast, scrap iron for dinner and matches for supper,—but I draw the line at gin! If my physician thinks that the interior of my anatomy needs blasting out, let him load me up with powder, with gun-cotton, with dynamite—I draw the line at gin! A healthy boy will never convince me that he starts out with an appetite for such stuff!

III. The hour demands action along legal lines. We have made much progress in temperance education, but the drink traffic under the fostering influences of excise laws seems to have grown in power for evil from day to day.

Here we find progress in the wrong direction except in two or three States, where the saloon has been abolished.

A man was released from Sing Sing the other day who had been confined there thirty-three years. The progress of the world in those years is a constant source of amazement to him. He walks the streets of New York, a feeble old man now, and can scarcely recognize the great metropolis with its three millions of people as the town he left thirty-three years ago. Within that time, the nation has been baptized in blood, and millions of slaves made freemen. Kingdoms have risen and fallen. The map of Europe has been made over again. The hum of a thousand new industries, and the flash of the electric light speak of a new age and a new civilization. In one thing he found no improvement. In the year 1855 in a drunken brawl in a saloon he had killed a man. With a shudder of horror he saw the same red lights of the saloon throwing their hellish glare across the pathway of his broken life! He finds it even more difficult now than in 1855 to get beyond the range of the saloon!

There are those who say this is none of my business. Well, in one sense it is not. But in another it is. Coming into the city the other day from the seashore, as our train dashed by a village crossing, it suddenly gave a sharp lurch and quickly came to a halt. In a moment more we were rapidly backing up to the station. I looked out and saw a great crowd gathering. With the others I rushed to the spot and saw on the stones beside the track the mangled body of a little nine-year-old girl. The bloody trunk lay upon one side of the rails and the ghastly head upon the other. The limbs and muscles were still spasmodically moving in the agonies of death. In a moment or two our whistle sounded and we were again rattling on toward the city. As our train pulled out, the mother came upon the scene, and above all other sounds rang her wild cry of despair! I heard it above the roar and rattle of engine and cars and I can hear it yet! It was strictly none of my business. It was not my child. But it was my privilege to weep! I had the right to look away out the window at the leaden sky and with that broken-hearted mother to cry! Yes, in a higher sense it *was* my business. The cry of suffering humanity is always the trumpet call of God! If we love God and our fellow-men we must respond to that call. And I shall ever consider it my duty to use my influence to abolish grade-crossings, remembering that bloody scene.

I am told that the remedy I must apply is moral suasion. I believe in moral suasion, but I believe in the exercise of common sense as to when it should be applied. A man passing a jungle is attacked by a ferocious tiger. His arm is being crushed between the jaws of the brute. Nerve and muscle and artery and bone are being ground between those teeth as he drinks the rich life blood. What must the traveller do now? Use moral suasion on the beast? Must he stroke him gently on the head with his disengaged hand and say in soothing tones, "Come, let me reason with you, tiger; I appeal to your judgment, that it is unfair and unkind and wrong for you to chew my arm in that style!" Should he do this? And at the same time should his fellow-traveller who stands by, draw near and use all his powers of persuasion to convince his stricken friend that it is altogether unseemly to allow himself to be eaten up in such a manner? Is this what we mean by moral suasion?

In our present situation we have need of another method first. The stricken traveller draws his knife and plunges it to the hilt into the body of the brute that attacks him, and this prepares the way for the application of gentler methods later. So we need legal suasion first, to be supplemented by moral suasion.

The open saloon I challenge as a wild beast, that still prowls with blood-stained claws and teeth along the highways of the nineteenth century. It has no mission save to murder and destroy that which is good, true, and beautiful in our life.

I arraign and indict the open saloon before

the court of public conscience, in the name of God and humanity, as the arch fiend and chronic criminal of modern civilization. In my bill of indictment there are five counts against the accused, either one of which is sufficient to condemn him to penal servitude in a warmer climate than this forever.

First—The open saloon is the manufacturer of criminals, and therefore cannot be legalized, save by an act of suicide on the part of the state. Drunkenness is a crime. If a policeman finds a man on the street, whose breath is loud and knees weak, does he rub him with St. Jacob's Oil for rheumatism? No, he whacks him over the head with a billy, thrusts him into a cart and dumps him into the station house for a season of rest. Is it right for the state to punish the drunkard, and at the same time offer a premium to those who make him drunk and kick him out into the street to stagger and mutter and caricature a man till arrested?

A short time ago it was declared by one of our daily papers that Police Justice Welde was also the owner of a saloon. The press went into hysterics over the announcement. How outrageous, that a man should make his fellow drunk at night, pocket the proceeds, and in the morning sentence him to the Island for getting drunk over his bar to which he had been lured! Truly such would be a most scandalous situation. But strange it is, that it does not occur to people that this is precisely the case with the whole license system. Police Justice Welde does not sit on the judge's bench as an individual. He is the representative of the sovereign State of New York. His individuality has nothing to do with his judicial duties. He is not known as an individual, nor is he allowed to know individuals in his official duties. He simply represents the State. Likewise the saloon-keeper on the corner does not sell as an individual. He is the representative of the State, and can only sell when he shows his commission—delegating from the State the authority to officially and legally act as its representative. He is merely the creature of the State, the general treasury receiving the profits of the business jointly with him. It in nowise changes the situation when you make the same individual the owner of the bar and the judge on the bench—for in both cases it is the State that acts. The principle remains the same. But why did people hold up their hands in holy horror at this incident? Because it was a concrete illustration of the basal principle of the license system, which has been hitherto overlooked, but in this case stood out in all its hideous deformity. The meaning of it all is that at heart the people are right, and when they once really do understand the true inwardness of the license business, there is already enough righteous dynamite under it to blow it back into the dark ages where it belongs! God speed the day!

Second—The open saloon is the rendezvous of criminals—criminals against government and outlaws from society. It is the home of red-handed anarchy. There are five or six Sunday-schools in Chicago in which Anarchists teach their children the gospel according to

John Most and the devil. Where are those schools held? In the saloons. No other roof would give shelter to such a devilish brood. The saloon is the school into which our foreign population is first dragged, and taught to curse religion, the Bible, God, the Sabbath, home, and all law. It is the open slaughter pen in which are butchered shame, manhood, honor, ambition, love. Is it right to legalize such an institution, or offer a premium for its management? You may say we cannot make men religious or sober by legislation. Perhaps so; but in God's name I protest against making them drunk by legislation. If you cannot make a man sober by law, then in the sacred name of law, give no more legal permits to make them drunk.

Third—The open saloon forces on the market at least forty per cent more liquors than the appetite of the public, even in its present degenerate condition, could consume without its allurements. It has been asserted again and again by the liquor trade that more is sold under prohibition than license, and this, their own statement, they invariably prove to be a lie by their frantic efforts to defeat prohibition and secure its repeal whenever enacted. This assertion, I remember, was made last year in Raleigh, N. C., by Northern liquor dealers, who were there with their money and agents, belying their words by paying $5 a head for votes for license. When the first saloon was opened, after two years of prohibition, men enough could not be placed behind the bar to accommodate the customers. Three carloads of liquors, it is said, were consumed within thirty-five hours, showing that the supply had not been equal to the demand.

Senator Ingalls, speaking of the results in Kansas of prohibition, says in the *Forum* for August, 1889:

"But the habit of drinking is dying out. Temptation being removed from the young and the infirm, they have been fortified and redeemed. The liquor-seller, being proscribed, is an outlaw, and his vocation is disreputable. Drinking being stigmatized, is out of fashion and the consumption of intoxicants has enormously decreased. Intelligent and conservative observers estimate the reduction at ninety per cent; it cannot be less than seventy-five."

Fourth—Public sentiment can never be educated in true temperance sentiment while the saloon is open and protected by the law. The liquor business is too respectable by far, these people are too often received into society in which good and true people mingle, and are even received by the Roman Catholic church, and in exceptional instances some others. How the whiskey men groan that prohibition drives the whole business to low-down channels—that mean low-down men are then engaged in it. Exactly so; and that is just what we want. I want to see mean men only engaged in it. The meaner a man is, the better qualified a man is for the business anyway. We want to drive it into the back alleys, cellars, and dark holes, where only the desperate and devilish will sneak to get it. Less respectable indeed! We want to make it bite the dust and crawl in the dirt, mud, and filth. Make it crawl, crawl, crawl in the ditch, in the gutter, in the sewer, and on into hell where it belongs!

Fifth—It is asserted that under prohibition any man can get drunk that wants to—well, any fool knows that—but I charge the open saloon with giving this poison to thousands who don't want it. We cannot protect those who want it, and will have it—we can save those who don't want it, and yet now have it thrust under their nose. You can save the honest workingman, who at eventide must walk by those open doors through which float the sounds of music and revelry that entice him in. You can save the noble young from the allurements of such legalized resorts, made bright and attractive with tinsel and obscenity in print and picture. To carry no-license is not the end of temperance work; it is but the beginning of the fight for the mastery of the young mind and life: it is the silencing of the battery of the enemy, and the opening of our own—the beginning of a victorious ending! Can we be indifferent to such a work?

Will we ever succeed in closing the saloons?

Let no man who loves God and humanity for a moment despair. We are as sure to succeed as that God lives, and that truth and right will prevail. Prohibition has recently been defeated in New Hampshire, Massachusetts, Rhode Island, and Pennsylvania. But these defeats are in reality victories. The saloon is simply piling up wrath against the day of wrath. The vast majority of the voters of America are to-day opposed to the saloon. It will only take a few more years for the high license idea to fizzle out. In the hearts of many good people this high license blunder is yet firmly fixed. But they will see clearly by-and-by, and then—the flood comes! The saloon power has succeeded, just now, in damming the flow of prohibition waters. They have placed another layer on the dam in Pennsylvania, when the waters were about to break over—so they did in Massachusetts, and in New Hampshire, and in Rhode Island. But every inch higher they raise that dam only postpones for a while the more awful destruction that is sure to come. Behind the dam the water is slowly and noiselessly rising. Back up on the mountains, whose streams, pure and sparkling, pour their treasures into the valley, I hear the roll of distant thunder—it is the rising heart-beat of long-suffering humanity! Higher and higher those waters are climbing, adding ton on ton of hydraulic pressure. That dam is not solid. It is built of mud and filth and rubbish. It has been repaired, again and again in times of emergency, by stuffing glass bottles, newspapers, and greenbacks into the cracks. In the centre there is nothing solid—nothing that can withstand the mighty pressure of those climbing waters. By-and-by a storm of righteous indignation will sweep the nation, and every rivulet on hill and mountain-side will come plunging down into the valley a roaring torrent! And then the flood! Every saloon is built below that dam. And there will not be one left to tell the story of their fall! God speed the day!

JESUITISM.

I ABHOR denominational bickerings. I believe in religious liberty—the right of every man to worship God according to the dictates of his own conscience. This is one of the fundamental principles of Americanism. Jesuitism, however, is the negation of Americanism. Jesuitism means imperialism. Americanism means freedom. Jesuitism means the unconditional slavery of the individual to the machine. Americanism means the highest liberty of the individual. Jesuitism not only enslaves its own subjects, but seeks to throttle all who do not bow to its supremacy. For this reason I hate it.

This so-called *Society of Jesus* is not strictly a religious order, it is social and political in its foundation and purposes, and merely uses religion as one of the weapons with which to accomplish its ends. Secrecy is one of the cardinal principles of the order, deceit and hypocrisy among its favorite devices, for which ample apology is made in its codes. They are an organized band of conspirators, under the most thorough discipline and complete organization ever conceived by the mind of man. They believe in higher education, and have been, and are, the chief teachers of the Roman Catholic church. They have ever been animated by the highest ambitions. They once furnished the world with many of its most illustrious heroes and martyrs. They are made of stern material. They are terribly in earnest. The Jesuit is to-day supreme in the councils of Rome. He educates the priesthood and young manhood of the American Catholics. He is the supreme dictator of the methods of education adopted by this church. His principles are now promulgated by the Pope from the Vatican as the voice of God.

By reason of its growing power and influence in America, Jesuitism, it seems to me, is a menace to our country—a menace to individual liberty, religious liberty, and the freedom of the whole people.

I. I say this, first, because of the HISTORY OF THE ORDER.

From the Reformation, with Martin Luther as its leader, dates the birth of modern thought. The mind of man lay chained in the dungeons of ecclesiasticism. The Reformation set mind free, and man began to think. Here freedom was born. But the great wave of this revolution that swept like a cyclone over a part of Europe, produced also a counter wave in the Latin nations near by. While a Luther was born to Germany, Spain produced a Loyola. Loyola was the negation of Luther. Luther's life was given to freeing the world from the domination of the errors of the Dark Ages, and the dominion of the Pope. Loyola's life was given to the undoing of Luther's work, the reëstablishment of the absolute despotism, spiritual and temporal, of the Pope. Loyola was a general in the Spanish army. The order he founded was one run upon the sternest principles of military discipline, the complete merging of the individual into the machine. Absolute obedience to one supreme commander was the fundamental principle. His command, right or wrong, was to be obeyed as the voice of God.

His success was phenomenal. In a short time he was at the head of the most powerful organization in the world. He rescued France, Spain, Portugal, and Austria from the grasp of the Reformation. It has been well said that Luther moved Europe by ideas which emancipated the millions, and set in motion a progress which is the glory of our age; Loyola invented a machine which arrested this progress, and drove the Catholic world back again into the superstitions and despotisms of the Middle Ages.

The success of Jesuitism was due to the extraordinary virtues, abilities, and zeal of the early Jesuits and their wonderful machinery. After the first period of sacrifice and success, followed the period of power and wealth, and consequent corruption, in which the first ripened fruit was gathered from the tree which

Loyola had planted. Their ambitions knew no bounds. Slaves themselves to one supreme will, they sought to enslave the world they had conquered. Their principles at once clashed with all civil power, whose rights they refused to recognize, denying all allegiance to any state. For political reasons they were, therefore, expelled from Portugal in 1759; from Spain in 1767; from France in 1764; and finally in 1773 the society was dissolved by Pope Clement XIV., upon the united petition of all the Catholic nations of Christendom. But in 1814, Pope Pius VII. concluded that Clement had made a mistake (both of them infallible, however), and so he restored the order to its ancient foundations. The reason why Pius restored the order was a very simple one. Jesuitism had swallowed Roman Catholicism, and to oppose Jesuitism was to cut his own throat. Again they began operations, and again it became necessary to expel them from the principal nations of Europe. They were expelled from Switzerland in 1847; from Spain in 1868; from Germany in 1872;

and from France in 1880. Westward the star of empire takes its course, and these exiled priests have thronged to the shores of free America, and are here scheming and dreaming of new kingdoms and conquests. They are doing to-day, what they always have been doing, what they always must be doing, plotting and scheming, plotting and scheming to stop the progress of civilization, and enslave mankind, until all bow and kiss the big toe of some feeble old Italian, who has the effrontery to call himself infallible and the vicegerent of God on earth!

II. Because of their principles and doctrines, the Jesuits are a menace to our country. Where there is the highest development of liberty, there is always a danger of a counter-current, a reaction—so is Jesuitism the counter-current of Americanism.

1. These men are politically against our institutions, and can never be amalgamated with our people. They are the serfs of a foreign feudal lord. They are the slaves of a foreign master. They take a solemn oath to put

themselves in the hands of their superior commander *as a corpse*, with no will or thought of their own. Each one, among other things in his oath, swears: " I do renounce and disown any allegiance as due to any heretical King, Prince, or State named Protestant, or obedience to any of their inferior magistrates or officers."

2. Their fundamental political doctrine is that the Church (Roman Catholic) is above the State, which is nothing short of high treason. This is the corner stone of their educational and religious system. In 1870 they forced on the Romish church the dogma of the Pope's infallibility—an error that has had an overwhelming influence in shaping the policy of the church. To show their triumph I quote some recent declarations from the highest Catholic authorities.

Bishop Gilmour in his Lenten Letter, March, 1873, said: " Nationalities must be subordinate to religion, and we must learn that we are Catholics first and citizens next. God is above man, and the church above the state."

Cardinal Manning put the following sentences in the mouth of the Pope: "I acknowledge no civil power; I am the subject of no prince; and I claim more than this. I claim to be the supreme judge and director of the consciences of men; of the peasant that tills the fields, and of the prince that sits upon the throne; of the household that lives in the shade of privacy, and the legislator that makes laws for kingdoms; I am the sole, last, supreme judge of what is right and wrong." He also says: "Moreover, we declare, affirm, define, and pronounce it to be necessary to salvation for every human creature to be subject to the Roman Pontiff." Of the utter degradation of reason, and the stifling of conscience the teaching of Cardinal Bellarmine affords a good example: "If the Pope should err by enjoining vices or forbidding virtues, *the Church would be obliged to believe vices to be good and virtues bad*, unless it would sin against conscience."

3. The doctrines of Jesuitism are subversive of true morality and destructive of the very

foundations of character. I can only quote a few of these doctrines as illustrations. The Parliament of Paris on March 5th, 1762, in a decree against the Jesuits drew up the following indictment which has never been successfully questioned:

"These doctrines, the consequence of which would destroy natural law, that rule of morality which God himself has implated in the hearts of men, and, consequently, would break all the ties of civil society, in authorizing theft, lying, perjury, the most criminal impurity, and generally all passions and all crimes, by the teaching of secret compensation, of equivocation, of mental restrictions, of probabilism and philosophical sin; destroy all feelings of humanity among men, in authorizing homicide and parricide, annihilate royal authority, etc."

We must remember that this was the official utterance of a Roman Catholic nation through its Parliament assembled. An examination of their doctrines as taught to-day, shows the fact that they are substantially the same doctrines taught in 1762. See "THE DOCTRINES OF THE JESUITS," published by B. F. Bradbury & Co., Boston, Mass., which is a translation of the works of Father Gury, S. J., Professor of Moral Theology in the College Romain of France.

Hear Father Gury on the celebrated doctrine of *mental reservation:*

"A culprit interrogated judicially, or not lawfully by the judge, may answer that he has done nothing, meaning 'about which you have the right to question me,' or, 'that I am obliged to avow.'

This mode of restriction may be used by all public functionaries questioned on things confided to their discretion; or secretaries, ambassadors, generals, magistrates, lawyers, physicians and all those who have reasons to hide some truth relative to their charge.

You must keep a *confided* secret, even if you are questioned about it by a superior, a judge, etc. You must answer them: "I do not know anything about it," because that knowledge is for you absolutely as if it did not exist; and thus should the secret be confided expressly or tacitly." ("Treatise on the Seventh and Tenth Precepts of the Decalogue," Articles 443, 444, 472.)

As to stealing we have this:

"Question. Must one always be considered guilty of theft when he takes the property of his neighbor?" How simply God's word answers: "Thou shalt not steal!" But hear the Jesuit's answer! "It may happen that the one from whom the property is stolen has no right to be opposed to the theft: which takes place, for instance, when the one who takes what belongs to his neighbor is in extreme need; and when he takes only what he badly needs; *or when he takes it secretly, as a compensation*, not being able to secure in a different way what is owed him by right of justice." Under such teaching we need not wonder that servants should "compensate" themselves secretly at their employer's expense.

III. The Jesuit is a menace to our country because of what he is now doing the world over—and what they mean to do in America in particular. They lead the Catholic church in its aggressions upon the liberties of mankind in all nations. Every Cardinal, archbishop and bishop of the Catholic church now takes an oath of allegiance to the Pope, in which occur the following words: "Heretics, schismatics, and rebels to our said lord (the Pope), or his aforesaid successors, I will to my utmost persecute and oppose." Rome is tolerant in America simply because she is not yet strong enough to be intolerant.

Says Bishop O'Connor: "Religious liberty is merely endured until the opposite can be carried into effect without peril to the Catholic world." *The Catholic Review* says: "Protestantism, of every form, has not, and never can have, any right where Catholicity is triumphant." The Archbishop of St. Louis once said: "Heresy and unbelief are crimes; and in Christian countries, as in Italy and Spain, for instance, where all the people are Catholics, and where the Catholic religion is an essential part of the law of the land, they are punished as other crimes."

Another Catholic writer of high authority, much petted at Rome, Mr. Louis Veuillot, puts it in a nutshell thus:

"When there is a Protestant majority we

claim religious liberty, because such is their principle; but when we are in majority we refuse it, because that is ours."

In accordance with these principles we see a Protestant minister arraigned in Spain last year for the crime of denying that the *image* of the " Virgen de los Dolores " had any power to heal diseases. Hear the sentence of the court.

" For this sacrilege of 'comparing,' as the court says, the sacred image of the Virgen de los Dolores with the manger of the horse of the priest, and attributing the same virtue to this miserable object as to that, by which the greatest scorn is thrown upon the *worship* of the holy images, etc., Pastor Vila is condemned to two years, four months and one day of imprisonment; to pay a fine of two hundred and fifty *pesetas* ($50), and the costs of court."

We turn to Mexico and hear President Diaz thus address the last Congress:

" This progress has indeed been praiseworthy because of the determined opposition of the Catholic clergy, sworn enemies of all civilization, who have always tried to stop the intellectual flight of free peoples." Further on he said:

"The Catholic clergy of Mexico, united in fatal concubinage with a faction of unworthy Mexicans, have thrice betrayed their country. In each case their crime was generously forgiven, though not forgotten by the republic. First, in the glorious days when independence was won, the traitorous clergy, forming alliance with the nation's conquerors and using excommunion as a weapon, hindered for eleven years the attainment of liberty. A second time, during the celebrated period of reform, the clergy joined the country's enemies. A third time traitorous, in the French usurpation, they helped set up a foreign monarchy on Mexican soil."

What are they doing in America? Building colleges, schools, and churches, pulling political wires in the cities, the States, the nation, and crushing the last spark of free thought that may linger in the breasts of their American priesthood. Father Lambert, of Waterloo,

N. Y., was driven to Rome, and driven back in disgrace, simply because he dared to think. Dr. McGlynn, was driven out of his church, excommunicated, and cursed, simply because he was guilty of a little thought outside the beaten tracks of theological and ecclesiastical dogmas. He was informed that he had no right to think for himself; and for pitying the woes of humanity, and for advocating what seemed to him a remedy, he was crushed by the machine. He was too big a man to be annihilated by such a process, however. The machine has lost his power, and freedom has gained a new champion.

Cardinal Gibbons reads us a lession in *catholicity* by calling on freemen of the nineteenth century to curse Giordano Bruno for daring to be a philosopher, for daring to think, when forbidden by the machine of the Middle Ages to do so. He says it is a crime and outrage that Bruno's friends should dare to build a monument to his memory on the spot where he was burned to death by order of Rome. Poor Bruno has been dead nearly three hundred years, and yet the Cardinal, who poses now as the champion of liberty, calls on free American citizens to curse his memory and his followers who yet survive. So does the Cardinal thus indorse his brutal murder. Truly Rome does not seem to change on some points at least! Does the Cardinal mean to imply by his tirade against Bruno and his friends that he would dare to re-enact that horrible tragedy on American soil if he had the power?

Does Cardinal Gibbons, the highest and most liberal representative of the Romish machine, believe in religious liberty? Let us turn to his book and see. We turn to page 264 and read his definition: "A man enjoys *religious* liberty when he possesses the free right of worshipping God according to the dictates of a RIGHT conscience, and of practising a form of religion most in accordance with his duties to God." A "right" conscience, as he elsewhere shows, is a Roman Catholic conscience, and *the only* "form of religion most in accordance with duty to God" he shows elsewhere to be the Roman Catholic religion.

Strictly within the bounds of that definition he could re-enact the horrors of the reign of Alva in the Netherlands, repeat the massacre of St. Bartholomew, reorganize the Spanish Inquisition, rekindle the martyrs' fires, and again sing a *Te Deum* over it all! The Cardinal boasts that Lord Baltimore, a Roman Catholic, granted religious liberty to Maryland. Perhaps he did. But in that far he failed to be a good Romanist according to this definition. If Baltimore did champion religious liberty, he did not learn his lesson from such a teacher as the Cardinal, and he granted this liberty, not by reason of, but in spite of, his religion, if we are to judge by such authorities.

We need not wonder, then, that a short time ago, in Maryland, a young girl was arrested at the dictation of a priest and dragged before a civil magistrate, whose only crime consisted in the fact that she had professed conversion and joined a Baptist church. In spite of all that could be done for her defence, through the machinations of this priest and a drunken father, she was sentenced to a term of penal servitude in a Catholic reformatory. And this happened in the city of Baltimore beneath the shadow of the Cardinal's palace! Times seem to have changed since the days of his Lordship, the founder of the colony!

A talented young Southerner, a citizen now of New York City and a member of the most powerful political organization in the metropolis, told me voluntarily the other day, that the more he saw of the management of the politics of New York, the more clearly he saw the hand of the Jesuit, and the more he trembled for the future of the Republic.

Their great university is located at the capital of the nation solely for political reasons. They have their hands with more or less power on every great daily newspaper in the United States. They know that America holds the destiny of the world and they mean to conquer America. Does any man think that the hierarchy has grown more liberal in modern times, and that the liberties of mankind could be safely intrusted in their hands? If so, let him read the encyclical that was sent to America last year from Leo XIII., the present Pope. This letter was received as the voice of God. It was reprinted in a Baltimore paper and a leading Protestant minister of the city openly challenged Cardinal Gibbons to give an explanation of it that would harmonize it with our Constitution! The Cardinal did not respond. And why? Because there was no possible explanation to be given. Its whole spirit and letter is the very negative of our fundamental laws—the denial of the principles on which our Republic is built. The subject of this encyclical, strange to say, is "Human Liberty." Now as to civil liberty, here is a part of what the Pope says:

"For, once granted that man is firmly persuaded of his own supremacy, it follows that the efficient cause of the unity of civil society is to be sought, not in any principle exterior or superior to man, but simply in the free-will of individuals; that the power of the state is from the people only; and that, just as every man's individual reason is his only rule of life, so the collective reason of the community should be the supreme guide in the management of public affairs. Hence the doctrine of the supremacy of the majority, and that the majority is the source of all law and authority. But, from what has been said, it is clear that all this is in contradiction to reason."

As to liberty of speech we have this revelation: "From this it follows, that greatly opposed to reason, and tending absolutely to pervert men's minds, is that liberty of which we speak, in so far as it claims for itself the right of teaching what it pleases—a liberty which cannot be granted by the state without failing in its duty. And the more so, because the authority of the teacher has great weight with his hearers, who can rarely decide for themselves as to the truth or falsehood of the instruction given to them." . . . "To this society, the Church, He intrusted all the truths which He had taught, that it might keep and guard them, and with lawful authority explain them; and at the same time He commanded all nations to hear the voice of the Church, as if it were His own, threatening those who would not with everlasting perdition." . . . "In faith and in the teaching of morality, God made the Church a partaker of His divine authority, and through His divine help she cannot be deceived. She is therefore the greatest and most safe teacher of mankind, with inviolable right to teach them."

That is to say, he would if he could, and will as soon as he can, close every Protestant church, silence every Protestant preacher, and compel every member to accept the teachings of the Romish church. And this should be done by the strong arm of the law. Hear him:

"False doctrines, than which no mental plague is greater, and vices which corrupt the heart, should be diligently repressed by public authority lest they insidiously work the ruin of the state."

And in his summary, lest he should be misunderstood by some careless reader, the Pope reaffirms his position in language whose meaning cannot be mistaken:

"From what has been said, it follows that it is in no way lawful to demand, to defend, or to grant unconditional freedom of thought, of speech, of writing, or of religion, as if they were so many rights which nature had given to man."

Let us remember that this letter does not bear the date of the Dark Ages, though each words drips with the congealed ignorance, arrogance, and bigotry of the darkest of the Dark Ages—no, my countrymen, it is dated Rome, A.D. 1888.

The learned De Tocqueville, from Catholic France, predicts, in his great book on America, that if the American Republic ever falls it will be at the hands of the Roman Catholic clergy. Certainly if they believe such stuff as this we have quoted to be the voice of God, it will be well to maintain an eternal watch over the liberties we have won through so much blood. I do not fear the result of any conflict that may come, but it is time our people were beginning to open their eyes to the fact that it is coming.

THE SCHOOL WAR.

THE *Boston Herald* relates the fact that Mr. Matthew Arnold was struck by the democratic government of the reading-room when he was in Boston. He came in one day and saw a little barefooted newsboy sitting in one of the best chairs of the reading-room, enjoying himself apparently for dear life. The great essayist was completely astounded. "Do you let barefooted boys in this reading-room?" he asked. "You would never see such a sight as that in Europe. I do not believe there is a reading-room in all Europe in which that boy, dressed as he is, would enter." Then Mr. Arnold went over to the boy, engaged him in conversation, and found that he was reading the "Life of Washington," and that he was a young gentleman of decidedly anti British tendencies, and for his age remarkably well informed.

Mr. Arnold remained talking with the youngster for some time, and, as he came back to the desk, the great Englishman said: "I do not think I have been so impressed with anything else that I have seen since arriving in this country as I am now with meeting this barefooted boy in this reading-room. What a tribute to democratic institutions it is to say that instead of sending that boy out to wander alone in the streets, they permit him to come in here and excite his youthful imagination by reading such a book as the "Life of Washington"! The reading of that one book may change the whole course of that boy's life, and may be the means of making him a useful, honorable, worthy citizen of this great country. It is, I tell you, a sight that impresses a European not accustomed to your democratic ways."

Mr. Arnold here touched the secret of our power. America has long been the wonder of modern times to Europeans. How we have attained such heights of power and glory as a nation, with a mob government as they call it;

how the Republic has stood the strain of over a hundred years, the shock of the bloodiest civil war in the records of the world, and is to-day the mightiest nation of earth, is to them a constant source of amazement. The secret of it is, our fathers built the Republic on free boys and free brains!

Against this system of broad republican education the Romish hierarchy has made a most deadly assault. Our American system of free schools they have sworn to destroy, and to never sleep so long as there shall remain one stone upon another to its very foundations. Understand me, I say the hierarchy, the Romish machine, has made this assault. This war on our public schools was not inaugurated by the Roman Catholic citizens of America. On the other hand it was forced on them against their will by the men who set themselves up as the supreme directors of the consciences of men. The ecclesiastical machine has seized the American Catholic people by the throat, pried their mouths open, and are trying to ram their sectarian school system down their throats! They have used their church organization to form a gigantic conspiracy to this end, that covers the length and breadth of our country.

To accomplish their purposes two methods of attack are used. First, to withdraw all Roman Catholic children from the public schools, and place them in sectarian parochial schools under the immediate control of priests, nuns, and monks, and then to demand a division of the public school fund for the support of these so-called educational establishments. Second, when this cannot be done, or until it is done, they attempt to control by manipulations of various sorts the management of our public schools, mutilating text-books to suit their tastes, eliminating entirely obnoxious histories and other books, and controlling the appointment of teachers. In these secret assaults they seek to weaken the hold of the public school on the hearts of the people, and to defeat the purpose of its existence, which is to give a full, free, broad, liberal education. To this end, therefore, they attack the public schools because the King James version of the Bible was read at its opening—saying that this is a Protestant Bible and makes the schools sectarian. They have succeeded in many places in banishing the Bible from the public schools, and no sooner was this accomplished than they turn and denounce anew these schools because they are "secular," "godless," "infidel!" Showing that their purpose from the beginning has been to *destroy* not to *reform* the public school. This issue about the reading of the King James Bible is a side skirmish they have engaged in, to merely hide the real point of conflict. The friends of free education must not be deceived by it. We can afford to yield this issue without a struggle, for the purpose of our public school is not to teach religion—the state has no right to teach religion of any sort—and we have no right to force our version of the Bible upon the child of the Jew or Catholic who helps support these public state schools. The hue and cry about our schools being godless and infidel, because the Bible is not read at the opening, is the merest tomfoolery! As Prof. Fisher has pointedly said, we cannot call a bank a "godless" or an "infidel" institution because it does not open each morning with a chapter from the Bible. Religion must be taught at home and at church if it is to reach the heart and life. I went to a private school in childhood that made a specialty of religion. We read copiously from the Bible and repeated the ten commandments backward and forward. The result on my childish mind was merely the confusion of real religion with its outward forms and the growth in my heart of a contempt for it all. For my own part, I have always felt that such tampering with sacred things was a dangerous experiment. The history of nations whose public-school system has been sectarian has overwhelmingly confirmed in me this conviction. Dr. W. T. Harris, on this point, has well said:

"The utmost care should be taken to surround religious instruction with the proper atmosphere. The time and place should be made to assist instead of distracting the religious impression. With regard to the example of Germany, Austria, and other states, that place religious lessons on the regular school programme so many hours in a week, I boldly appeal to the experience of all who have inspected the results of such teaching, and inquire whether they do not confirm the theoretical conclusions here deduced. Do not the pupils, well taught in secular studies, learn to hold in contempt the contents of religious lessons? Do they not bring their critical intellects to bear on the dogmas, and become sceptical of all religious truths? Is not the Germany of to-day the most sceptical of all peoples? Is not its educated class famous for its 'free thinking,' so called? Then there is France, where the church had its own way with religious instruction until recently. Is there another class of people in the world so abounding in atheism as the French educated class? In other countries where religion is taught in the schools, does not the authoritative and dogmatic method of religion do much to render inefficient the instruction in the secular studies? Is not this apt to be the case in parochial schools?"

So also they have sought to control school boards and dictate the management of the public system. In Boston last year I had the honor to be a member of the Committee of One Hundred who managed the campaign for free education in that city. We found upon investigation that the school board, which had control of all the common schools of the city, Primary, Grammar, Latin, High, and Normal, was composed of twelve Catholics, eleven Protestants and one Jew; that all the important sub-committees within this board were controlled by a Catholic majority; that the committee on the nomination of teachers was composed of four Catholics and one Protestant; that this whole board was being practically managed by a coterie of Jesuit priests, who examined and passed upon the text-books that should be used; that at their dictation several standard books had been removed from the schools without a word; that again and again had competent Protestant teachers been removed without cause and incompetent Catholic teachers put in their places, and instruction sent to the superintendents that if complaints were made they would lose their positions. When Mr. Travis was removed from his chair of history, and Swinton's Outlines thrown out of the schools at the command of a priest by this servile board, is it any wonder that it precipitated a storm of public indignation that overturned the city government and reorganized that board? Scores of patriotic Catholic citizens voted the ticket of the Committee of One Hundred, and there are scores of such men in every city who will be found the champions of our free schools against all enemies.

But the method on which the hierarchy lay most stress and depend most for ultimate victory, is the first mentioned, this second one being merely tributary to the main object—namely to build a system of sectarian schools with the public fund now used in the maintenance of our free schools. This purpose is now at last boldly asserted by the hierarchy and is being pushed with remorseless persistency. Not a legislature meets at Albany that is not besieged by those who seek to divide the school fund for sectarian purposes. Sometimes the bill introduced bears one name, sometimes another—it is always the same old Trojan horse with this assassin of the free schools concealed within. It is asserted that the State of New York through its Assembly has already been robbed of over twelve million dollars of the people's money that has been given to sectarian institutions. That we may understand clearly the purpose of the Romish hierarchy in this matter, let us consult their authorities.

The *Catholic World* for October, 1889, has its leading article on this subject, entitled "A Canadian Example." The whole purpose of the article is to show that the only solution to our school question is the division of the school fund on a sectarian basis.

The Catholic *Review* of August 25th has the following pointer on the public-school question:

" The parochial school has come to stay.

And it means one day, without infringing on the public school in any way, to have the support of the State."

Says the *Freeman's Journal*, a Roman Catholic paper, in a recent issue: "This is why Catholics ask that the State let them educate their own children in their own way, with their own share of the school tax."

The Cincinnati *Catholic Telegraph*, insolently and exultingly shouts, "It will be a glorious day for the Catholics in this country when under the blows of justice (?) and morality (?) our school system shall be shivered to pieces."

The Roman Catholic priest, Monsignor Capel, according to a newspaper report of a conversation, which was widely circulated and never contradicted, said, "The time is not far away when the Roman Catholics, at the order of the Pope, will refuse to pay their school tax, and will send bullets to the breasts of the government agents, rather than pay it." "The order can come any day from Rome." "It will come as quickly as the click of the trigger, and it will be obeyed, of course, as coming from God Almighty himself."

The question is, Can we, as free Americans; can we, as Protestants; can we, as patriotic Catholic citizens, ever agree to those demands of the hierarchy?

I. I say we cannot, first, because these demands are based on false principles that attack the very foundations of our liberties and free institutions. These demands are based on the assertion that the Church (Roman Catholic) is above the State, and has the supreme and sole right to educate; that the priest is the supreme master of the citizen. This idea of ecclesiastical supremacy is simply centuries out of date. It comes to us from the gloom of the Dark Ages smelling of the dust and mould of an oblivion into which the progress of mankind has long since kicked it. A Catholic bishop recently expressed this idea very tersely in reply to a committee from the parish who waited on him to ask if certain reforms within that parish could be carried out provided a majority of the members favored it. The bishop, drew himself up indignantly, glared at his questioner a moment, and replied: "I am the majority, Sir!"

The hierarchy in this fight pretend to champion the "rights" of parents—that the parent should not be coerced into sending the child to the public school. They mean rather that they demand the sole right to dictate to the parent what shall be done with the child. Do they allow any choice to a parent as to where the child shall go when withdrawn from the public schools? No, they say to the parent, "If you do not send your child to the parochial school, I will hurl against you the curse of the church, and deny you the right to sleep in 'consecrated' ground." Again and again have they used excommunion as a weapon with which to coerce public-spirited parents into submission. An Irishman who patronized the public schools of Charlestown, Boston, was so threatened by his priest. He consulted one of the school board as to what he should do. The gentleman advised him that he was a free American citizen and that he had the right to do as he pleased. He continued to disobey the priest. He called again on this gentleman in a dilemma for advice. He said the priest told him if he did not send his child to the parochial school he would turn him into a rat! The gentleman laughed and advised Pat to let his Reverence try the experiment. Soon afterward he saw the Irishman, and asked him how he was getting on. Pat replied: "Oi'me right, Sor, as yit! We still sind to the school—and oi told me old o'oman to kape a sharp look out, and if she saw a tail a growin', to kill the cat!" It is not the right of the parent the priest thus seeks to protect, but the right of the machine to dictate to the parent.

II. We cannot agree to these demands, because these parochial schools are not being built primarily for the purpose of giving an adequate education for the masses, but are being built for the first purpose of destroying our free educational system.

Let us consult Catholic authorities and see if this is not the case. An American, who was in Rome on one occasion, was astonished at the appalling ignorance of the people of Italy. Being an American, he was fool enough to believe in universal education, so he sought Cardinal Antonelli, the Papal Secretary of State, and asked him for an explanation of the situation. In the Cardinal's reply he said that he "thought it better that the children should grow up in ignorance than be educated in such a system of schools as the State of Massachusetts supports; that the essential part of education was the catechism; and while arithmetic and geography and other similar studies might be useful, they were not essential." (*Int. Rev.*, vol. 8, p. 293.)

The *catechism* the essential part of an education! And this from the Vatican, the headquarters of the parochial system! Dr. McGlynn, who claims to be still a good Catholic in principle, says on this point:

"The extraordinary zeal manifested for getting up these sectarian schools and institutions is, first of all, prompted by jealousy and rivalry of our public schools and institutions, and by the desire to keep children and other beneficiaries from the latter; and, secondly, by the desire to make employment for and give comfortable homes to the rapidly-increasing hosts of monks and nuns who make so-called education and so-called charity their regular business, for which a very common experience shows that they have but little qualification beyond their professional stamp and garb. It is not risking much to say that if there were no public schools there would be very few parochial schools, and the Catholic children, for all the churchmen would do for them, would grow up in brutish ignorance of letters; and a commonplace of churchmen here would be the doctrine taught by the Jesuits in Italy, in their periodical magazine, the *Civita Cattolica*, that the people do not need to learn to read; that all they need is bread and the catechism, the latter of which they could manage to know something of even without knowing how to read."

Victor Hugo, in his famous speech in opposition to Jesuit control of the education of France, uses these burning words:

"You claim the liberty of teaching. Stop; be sincere; let us understand the liberty you claim. It is the liberty of *not* teaching. You wish us to give you the people to instruct. Very well. Let us see your pupils. Let us see those you have produced. What have you done for Italy? What have you done for Spain? For centuries you have kept in your hands, at your discretion, in your school, these two great nations, illustrious among the illustrious. What have you done for them? I shall tell you.

. . . .

"Italy, which taught mankind to read, now knows not how to read. Yes! Italy is, of all the States of Europe, that where the smallest number know how to read.

"Spain, magnificently endowed Spain, which received from the Romans her first civilization; from the Arab her second civilization; from Providence, in spite of you, a world—America—Spain, thanks to you, rests under a yoke of stupor, which is a yoke of degradation and decay. Spain has lost the secret power it obtained from the Romans, the genius of art it had from the Arabs, the world (of America) it had from God; and in exchange for all that you have made it lose, it has received from you the INQUISITION; the Inquisition, which certain of your party try to-day to re-establish; which has burned on the funeral pile millions of men; the Inquisition, which disinterred the dead to burn them as heretics; which declared the children of heretics infamous and incapable of any public honors, excepting only those who shall have denounced their fathers. . . .

"This is what you have done for two great nations. What do you wish to do for France? Stop! you have just come from Rome! I congratulate you; you have had fine success there; you have come from gagging the Roman people, and now you wish to gag the French people. . . . Take care! France is a lion, and is alive." We may likewise add to meddling enemies of our schools, "Take care! America is a lion, and is alive!"

As a climax of consistency, look now at the sentence I quoted from the *Catholic Review* of August 25th: " Means one day, without infringing on the public school in any way, *to have the support of the State!*" Could mortal man conceive of a more monstrous absurdity! " Have the support of the State"—without infringing on the public school in any way! To the mixture of simplicity and cheek composing that sentence I can remember but one parallel, and that is the case of the county commissioners who resolved to build a new jail. They resolved, " 1st, to build a new jail; 2d, to build it out of the bricks used in the old one; 3d to keep the prisoners in the old one while they built the new one; 4th to build the new one on the site where the old one now stands!" To have capped the climax of asininity they should have added as a final clause " without infringing on the old building in any way." Such a resolution thus concluded would have furnished a worthy companion piece to be framed and hung up in a museum alongside this marvellous proposition from the *Catholic Review!*

III. We cannot agree to these demands because the sectarian parochial school is narrow and bigoted, fosters class distinctions and hatreds, is anti-republican, and its standard of instruction is infinitely inferior to that of the public schools.

We have the best Catholic authority for saying they are inferior. The *Freeman's Journal and Catholic Register* for March 12th, 1887, complained of the parochial schools, where it said of the pupils: "A smattering of the catechism is supplied to fit them for the duties of life;" and intimated that the schools were only "apologies, compromises, systemless pretences."

Dr. Orestes A. Brownson, a distinguished Catholic, said of the Roman Catholic schools (*Brownson's Review*): "They practically fail to recognize human progress. . . . They do not educate their pupils to be at home and at their ease in their own age and country, or train them to be living, thinking, energetic men. . . .

They who are educated in our schools seem misplaced and mistimed in the world, as if born and educated for a world that had ceased to exist. . . . The cause of the failure of what we call Catholic education is, in our judgment, in the fact that we educate, not for the present or the future, but for the past. . . . an order of things which the world has left behind, for it could be reproduced, if at all, only by a second childhood."

The *Catholic Review*, April, 1871, gives to the world this revelation: "We do not indeed prize as highly as some of our countrymen appear to do, the ability to read, write, and cipher. Some men are born to be leaders, and the rest are born to be led. The best ordered and administered state is that in which the few are well educated and lead, and the many are trained to obedience," etc. Is it so!

And one of the most conclusive reasons why we know these schools to be inferior is that thousands of our most intelligent Catholic citizens defy the hierarchy and continue to patronize the public schools, because they know their superiority. It is no small thing for a Catholic to defy the governing clergy— it means often social ostracism, hatred, loss of friends and even the means of support.

It has been truly said, that the purpose of the sectarian parochial school is to make obedient Catholics, while the purpose of the public free school is to make good citizens. Now what is taught in these sectarian schools in many of their favorite text-books is anything but favorable to the production of a good citizen. It is often false and injurious in the highest degree to the mind and character of the child. They are constantly drilled in bigotry and hatred toward other denominations, with whom they are to live as citizens of a common government. They are taught to hate those they do not understand, and to avoid their presence. Let me quote from the "Catechism of Perseverance" one of their standard books published by T. B. Noonan & Co., of Boston, which has the approval of four bishops. I quote only the two final answers on the lesson in Chapter LIV.

"*Q.* How do you show that Protestantism, or the religion preached by Luther, Zuinglius, Calvin, and Henry VIII., is not the true religion?

"*A.* In order to show that Protestantism is a false religion, or rather no religion at all, it will be sufficient simply to bear in mind: 1st, that it was established by four great libertines; 2d, that it owes its origin to the love of honors, covetousness of the goods of others, and the love of sensual pleasures, three things forbidden by the Gospel; 3d, that it permits you to believe whatever you please and to do whatever you believe; 4th, that it has caused immense evils, deluged Germany, France, Switzerland, and England with blood; it leads to impiety, and finally to indifference, the source of all revolutions, past and future. We must, therefore, be on our guard against those who preach it, and cherish a horror for the books which disseminate it.

"*Q.* What religion is it that alone has rendered men better and alone has civilized them?

"*A.* The only religion which has rendered

men better and civilized them is the Catholic religion, to the exclusions of Arians, Mahometans, Protestants, and philosophers; the Catholic religion, therefore, alone is good, alone divine."

Bishop Gilmour's "Bible History" is a book very popular in these sectarian schools. Hear what this book says of the reign of the Tudors in England. The career of Bloody Mary is not mentioned at all and the account closes with this paragraph:

"Catholicity has ever appealed to reason; Protestantism, like Mohammedanism, to force and violence. In England and Scotland Protestantism was forced upon the people by fines, imprisonment, and death; in Germany and Prussia, Sweden, and Denmark and Norway, the same. In America the Puritans acted in like manner."

Catholicity has ever appealed to reason! Did Bishop Gilmour never read the edict with which Alva baptized the Netherlands in blood? This edict directed that all Protestants should be executed; the men with the sword, the women to be buried alive, provided they do not persist. That is, if they should recant they would be granted the sweet privilege of such a death—the women to be buried alive and the men to be butchered with the sword! But if they persisted they were to be burned with fire, and in either case all their property should be confiscated. The story of how this edict was executed is one of the most sickening chapters in the story of the human race. During the six years of Alva's reign, his executioners put to death 18,000 persons, besides the victims in cities captured by his troops and the hosts that fell in battle. Has the Bishop never read of the massacre of St. Bartholomew, the fires of the martyrs, or the Spanish Inquisition? I do not say that we are to teach these things in our public schools, but I do say that if the state must pay for instruction on these points, then the truth, the whole truth, and nothing but the truth must be taught!

Take their most popular geographies, published by Sadlier, Barclay street, New York, and used in most parochial schools. Let us take some three questions from the Lesson on the United States. The answers to these questions are fresh—they are startling news to most American citizens who thought they had a smattering at least of the history of their country.

"*Who were the first explorers of great portions of our country?*

" Catholic missionaries.

"*Who discovered and explored the upper Mississippi?*

" Father Marquette, a Jesuit missionary.

"*Where, in many of the States, were the first settlements formed?*

"Around the humble cross that marked the site of a Catholic mission." (Page 22, Lesson XXXII.)

Mr. Edwin Mead aptly remarks on this lesson:

" This is the general account of the colonization and early history of the United States. And this is a good sample of the proportion of the rôle assigned to Jesuit missionaries all through these books. You have heard of the boy who once asked his father, who was forever telling of his tremendous exploits at Bull Run and Gettysburg and Cold Harbor, "Father, did anybody help you put down the rebellion?" The descendant of the New England Puritans or of other worthies, whom some of us have been in the habit of thinking as standing for something in this American enterprise, is moved to ask the Jesuit, when he reads of all his accomplishments, in these books, "Did anybody help you found the American republic?"

As to New England in particular we have this historic revelation:

"*What was the first settlement in the New England States?*

"A Jesuit mission on Mount Desert Island (in 1612).

"*By whom was this settlement destroyed?*

" By the English.

"*What people made a permanent settlement in Massachusetts in 1620?*

" The Pilgrim fathers

"*Who were they?*

"English Protestants who, being persecuted by their Protestant fellow-countrymen, took refuge in America.

"*How did they act in their new home?*

"They proved very intolerant, and persecuted all who dared to worship God in a manner different from that which they had established."

Shall the public-school fund, levied and raised for the purpose of giving men and women an education that will fit them for the duties of life; shall this fund, the people's money, be devoted to the support of sectarian schools where monks and nuns teach such stuff as this? When this question is fairly before the American people, the answer will come as the roar of an earthquake to the ears of these meddling priests! Bismarck said that the saddest thing he saw in France was not the dead on battle fields, but mutilated and misleading text-books on the tables in Catholic schools. These books are scattered far and wide in these sectarian schools in America, doing their deadly work in the minds of our youth.

IV. We can never agree to the demands of

the hierarchy, because their plans successful would destroy our system of education, thus stabbing the Republic to the heart, and reunite Church and State.

To divide the school fund on a sectarian basis would not be simply a step toward the union of Church and State, it would be the consummation of actual union. Suppose you divide the fund on the per capita basis of the children. Directly into the hands of the ecclesiastical machine will fall millions of dollars. Does any candid intelligent man believe for a moment those ecclesiastics would devote these enormous sums to educational purposes? Simply the cost of the board and clothes of the hosts of monks and nuns who teach in these schools would be the extent of their expenditure. It would be inevitable that the money would go directly into the general treasury under the control of the bishop and be used for *church* purposes! We have already seen that this fight is not being made because of the zeal of the machine for popular education. The truth is, the prize for which this hierarchy is fighting so desperately, and promises to fight still more desperately, is the control of these munificent sums of money. When they get their hands on it, what will become of the schools? They will go where they have gone in Italy, in Spain, in Mexico, in South America—to the devil! where they have ever gone when the ecclesiastical machine has been master of popular education. A journal under their control said recently in a three-column article on this subject. "What, then, do Catholics want? Justice, absolutely nothing but justice, equal justice for all." He defines this "justice" to be a division of the school fund on a sectarian basis. This plea of injustice because parents are taxed for public-school purposes whose children go to private schools, I arraign as the climax of ignorance of our institutions and downright selfishness. To say the least, if it be not rebellion, it is a sad exhibition of unpatriotic sentiment. Besides there is not one spark of justice in such a demand. The school tax is not levied for the purpose of giving to the individual paying the tax an equivalent in education in his own family. The school fund is based upon a different principle entirely. Test the question and see. There are thousands of old bachelors in this country who are heavily taxed for school purposes. They receive no benefit in return in their immediate families. Then I demand justice for the old bachelors of this country! Divide the school fund! Give each old crusty wretch his share! There are thousands of old maids, too, who are taxed heavily for the support of the schools. Justice for the old maids! Divide the fund!

There are thousands of childless couples in this country who are taxed heavily to support public schools. They have no children in the schools. Divide the fund!

There are thousands of Baptists and Methodists and Presbyterians and others who patronize private schools exclusively who are taxed for the support of the public schools. "Equal justice for all!" Divide the fund! Give each crank a chromo for the maintenance of his crotchet! And let posterity take care of itself! "Posterity!"—what has posterity ever done for *us* anyhow!

Yes, such a man as this was he who refused to assist in the purchase of a new hearse for the village. The committee asked him why. He replied: "Well, I gave ten dollars to buy the old one, and neither I nor my family have ever had the use of it a single time!"

Such is the supreme selfishness of the man who would divide this fund raised for the common weal — a selfishness so cankerous that it fain would eat up the victim who proclaims it when other food has failed! This money is raised by the state as a life insurance fund. The life of the state rests on universal suffrage. Universal suffrage is a possibility only when supported by an universal education—and no such education has ever been given, or can be given save by the state.

Prate to me of individual rights here! Care you nothing for the life of this glorious free Republic, the asylum of all nations, the refuge of an oppressed world? Shall we allow it to be stabbed to the heart in a mad fight between sectarian brawlers?

We have no army, no navy worthy of the name, no frowning ramparts along our coasts to withstand the ironclads of the Old World, and yet we are the mightiest nation of earth—the last nation in all the roll of nations against which a foreign power will dare to draw the sword! And why? Because, we have not invested in steel guns, granite masonry or brass buttons, but in free boys and free brains! Shall the foundations of this glory be destroyed? Shall we re-enact the dismal failures of the Old World? The American people must answer. I have no fear as to what that answer will ultimately be. But it is time now that answer should begin to formulate itself in an overwhelming demand that in the Constitution of the United States and every State of the Union there shall be a clause, specifically forbidding that a single cent of the people's money shall ever be appropriated to sectarian purposes, either under the guise of charity or education.

THE SOUTHERN QUESTION.

SOME DIFFICULTIES OF THE SITUATION.

[An address before the New England Paint and Oil Club at their 44th dinner at the Hotel Thorndike, Boston, as reported by the *Boston Daily Herald*, April 14th, 1889.]

The 44th dinner of the Paint and Oil Club of New England, at the Thorndike, last evening, was attended by about fifty members and a dozen or more guests, among the latter being Rev. Thomas Dixon, Jr., pastor of the Dudley Street Baptist Church, and formerly a member of the North Carolina Legislature. An enjoyable reception of half an hour's duration was held in the parlors, after which the company repaired to the banquet hall, where an admirable dinner was served. The after-dinner speaking was inaugurated by President Daniel G. Tyler, who, in introducing the principal guest of the evening, said: "The Southern problem has been an interesting question to all close observers of national affairs since the war. Our guest this evening was born upon the soil of the Old North State, has served in her Legislature and in other posts of trust, and, after living in the North for a number of years, comes to-day to give us the benefit of his experience and thought upon the subject."

Rev. Mr. Dixon's Speech.

Rev. Thomas Dixon, Jr., on being thus pleasantly presented, spoke substantially as follows:

What do I mean by "The Southern Question?" Certainly not what the sectional monomaniac has in mind when he uses the expression. If by "Southern question" you mean the supposed problem of crime, violence, and semi-civilization, as presented in the cock-and-bull stories you hear of the South—then I have no time to discuss such a question, for such a problem exists only in the distorted fancy of ill-informed men. By "Southern question" I mean the sectional question, and the problem of it is, how can sectionalism be eliminated from our national life, social, economic, and political? If this is a union, unity should be the cardinal principle of national life, and sectionalism is a monstrosity. The South and North should stand related to each other, politically and commercially, as the Eastern, Western and Middle States are related.

What are some of the difficulties that stand in the way of such an obliteration of sectional lines? I can dwell on but two this afternoon.

1. Mutual misunderstanding. The North does not understand the South. The South does not understand the North. The ignorance of the average northerner as to the real condition of the South has been to me a constant source of amazement. What are the chief causes of these misunderstandings?

(*a*) The federal office-holders in the South under Republican administration. The concrete idea of the North has been presented to the South in the personality of the carpetbaggers, turncoat Democrats, and general rapscallions who have been honored with office under Republican Presidents. The most potent cry ever raised in the South on a national question was "Turn the rascals out." They meant the rascals at home, who used their offices to domineer over and insult the people whom they were placed there to serve. The civil service given the South, exept under Cleveland's administration, has been simply infernal. There have been some good men among them, but they were the exception to the rule. The finest stroke of policy yet made by President Harrison was when he sent home the other day the forlorn groups of chronic office holders and office seekers from South Carolina. Such a policy is a first step toward breaking a solid South.

(*b*) Cranks. Hot-headed, ill-advised men, thirsting for a sensation, and determined to make one, plunge into the South for a week or two, and return to the northern platform loaded with wind and exclamation points. They strut, and bellow, and shriek. "What are you going to do about it?" And sometimes the very elect are deceived by the noise into believing that something ought to be done! Such a D.D. recently spent a few weeks South. He returned with a pain he knew not where, with the griping sensation as yet unlocated, but with a determination to be heard or die. God save the South from her friends!

(*c*) Knaves. There are men who deliberately seek to deceive you on such questions. The day before the last election, the *New York Tribune* contained a long dispatch from Raleigh, N. C., stating that the town was in a state of riot and bloodshed; that the negroes were being driven from the place, shots were being exchanged and that there was urgent need of troops. Every word, every syllable, every letter, every dot on every i in the article was a lie out of whole cloth, as testified to by the mayor and council, among whom were four distinguished negro politicians.

(*d*) Politicians who trade in sectional issues only. The day for those men is rapidly going by. Some of them still remain, North and

South. Let the rising young men of the nation set their feet emphatically on all such.

(*e*) Partisan newspapers. It is a sad fact that we have so many newpapers in both sections whose business it seems to be to misrepresent each other and everything on the other side. Thousands of our best people read only these papers, and must, of necessity, see everything in a distorted light. They create and feed a morbid appetite for sensational and highly exaggerated matter on those questions. I am oftentimes disgusted at the attempt of our independent newspapers to straddle the universe on questions of grave importance to preserve their independence, yet with all their faults I thank God for them. They form to-day the only means of communication between the sections, and, it seems to me, mark an era in the progress of the nation. They have tempered the tone of our organs, so that they do not scream and bellow and rattle as of old, but must of necessity now give forth sounds more or less harmonious and reasonable. And the tune grows better as time rolls on.

2. The second great difficulty of the question I mention is, "The negro and his relation to the local governments of the South." The rising generation of the South never knew the negro as a slave and does not hate him because his skin is black. Why, then, do the young men, as well as the old men, stand as a unit in the determination that the negro shall not as yet control the local governments? Simply because they know he does not represent the wealth, virtue, and intelligence of the community, and because they know that negro supremacy in State or county means bankruptcy, ruin, disgrace, and corruption. I have no apologies to offer for the interference with the negro vote that has characterized certain sections of the South in times past. These things are mostly traditions now, and it is my earnest conviction, after living in New York and Boston, that there are as many crimes of one sort and another committed against the ballot in the North as in the South, taking the sections as a whole. But what was the cause then of intimidation and trickery in the South?

Take North Carolina as an example. Immediately on the enfranchisement of the hordes of ignorant slaves, and before the political disabilities of the whites were removed, the negroes, under the leadership of adventurers and villains, took possession of the state government and the county governments of about forty counties. They wrecked the state government in short order, stole everything they could get their hands on, even to the school fund, and the United States land script fund, issued millions of dollars worth of fraudulent bonds, raised what money they could on them and stole that. The governments of these forty counties were even more hopelessly wrecked. The county script was not worth the paper it was written on, and the land was taxed to nearly its full rental value, and land was the only capital the people had. What were the people to do in these forty black counties? Sell out and leave? They couldn't sell. Nobody would buy. Lands worth $20 an acre could not have been sold for fifty cents. **They did what you would have done—they took** possession of their local governments—they had to do it or give up the struggle of life. They violated the Constitution you say? Perhaps they did sometimes. But self-preservation is the first law of nature and antedates the Constitution somewhat. They said it was not right that pauperism and vice and ignorance should rule wealth and virtue and intelligence, and that all the constitutions of the earth couldn't make it right. After all, didn't you teach them the lesson? A distinguished senator of the North, when driven to the wall by the relentless logic of Calhoun on the Constitution, it is said, replied: "The Constitution be d—d!" The Constitution did stand between the slave and his freedom. You said it was not right, smashed it to atoms and made it over again. I thank you for doing it. You said the Constitution was not divine before the war. Could you expect these Southern men, whose very lives depended on the issue, to accept it as divine after the war?

This dark cloud of the possibility of local corruption and bankruptcy and ruin hangs like a pall over the South, and makes the white race stand together as a solid unit to-day. The enfranchisement of the negro race turned loose too much power. It forced the Southern people to go into politics rather than into business—their life depended on it. The white Republican party recently organized in Alabama is the dream of a fool. The white race cannot divide until the negroes first divide.

All this I say with the kindliest and tenderest feelings for the negro race. Yes, I say it by the memories of the dear old nurse in whose arms the weary head of my childhood so often found rest, at whose feet I sat and heard the sad story of the life of a slave until I learned to hate slavery as I hate hell.

What would I give as the solution of the Southern question? Pass the Australian ballot system or a good educational qualification for suffrage in every State in the Union, and it will disfranchise two-thirds of the negroes and one-third of the whites in the South, the terror of negro misrule will disappear, and with it, I believe, sectionalism.

www.ingramcontent.com/pod-product-compliance
Lightning Source LLC
Chambersburg PA
CBHW032148230426
43672CB00011B/2490